KA MOI

CLASS OF 1935

PRINCESS BERNICE PAUAHI BISHOP
1831-1884

HON. CHARLES R. BISHOP
1822-1915

MR. E. FAXON BISHOP

To Mr. E. Faxon Bishop, who, as the trusted friend of Mrs. Bishop
and of every student, has given a lifetime of devotion to the best
interests of the Kamehameha Schools, we dedicate this Annual.

SENIOR CLASS SONG

Words and Music by Class of '35,
Kamehameha School for Girls

"HOME NANI O KAMEHAMEHA"

Hiki anei ke kali iki iho makou,
  Ma na alahele uluwehi i na pua,
E kilohi e hoopa a e honi iho,
  Ika nani ou e Kamehameha.

Chorus:
Home nani e, Kamehameha e,
  Me kou mau puu uli e,
Na mauna omao i na laau,
  Homai kou mele kamahao no makou.

"BEAUTIFUL HOME OF KAMEHAMEHA"

Can't we linger a little while longer,
Among the paths of flowered bowers,
And stop to see and feel and smell,
The beauty of our Kamehameha Home.

Chorus:
Kamehameha, Home of beauty,
Kamehameha with your sweet scented hills,
Your stately mountains with ironwood trees,
Sing to us a wondrous song,
The clouds and rainbow overhead,
Pervades us with earth's riches,
We love our flowers and trees that grow,
Exhaling forth their sweet perfume,
We love our home upon the hill,
Where happy days ere were spent,
Memories that will never fade,
May they linger on,
May we dream and love forever,
Our Kamehameha Home of beauty.

Left—MISS MARGUERITE JUDSON
K. S. G. Senior Class Adviser

Right—MR. DONALD D. MITCHELL
K. S. B. Senior Class Adviser

CLASS MOTTO—Ka Hua O Ka Naauao,
Oia Ke Kumulaau O Ke Ola.

CLASS COLORS—Green and White

CLASS FLOWER—Gardenia

SENIOR CLASS OFFICERS

School for Boys

HERBERT DUNN . . . . President

JAMES NAKAPAAHU . . . . Vice President

JOSEPH ANUHEA . . . . Secretary

School for Girls

MARY KUNANE . . . . President

LENA SUPE . . . . Vice President

GLADYS NAONE . . . . Secretary

VIRGINIA WO . . . . Treasurer

ELLEN STEWART . . . . . Student Council Member

HAUNANI COOPER . . . . Student Council Member

MELE-ALLEN KEHAUNANI AINOA

"Not simple conquest, triumph is her aim."

HONOLULU, OAHU *mele a. Hooper 6-5-85*

ENTERED K. S. G. FROM SACRED HEART'S CONVENT, 1932

Teacher at Kalihi Union '35; Christian Endeavor Society '34; Garden Club '32, '33; '34; G. R. Senior Club '34; '35; Discussion Club '34; '35; Teacher at Castle Kindergarten '35.

IRENE EMMALANI AKEO

"As night the life-inclining stars best shows,
So lives obscure the starriest souls disclose."

KALAHEO, KAUAI

ENTERED K. S. G. FROM KALAHEO SCHOOL, 1932

Sunday School teacher at St. Mary's 35; Christian Endeavor Society '32, '33, '34; Garden Club '32, '33, '34; Girl Scouts '34, Color Bearer '35; Glee Club '33, '34, '35; Ka Moi Staff '33, '34, '35; Teacher at Castle Kindergarten '35.

MARJORIE KUUIPO ALO

"A word fitly spoken is like apples of gold in pictures of silver."

WAILUKU, MAUI

ENTERED K. S. G. FROM WAILUKU JUNIOR HIGH, 1932

Art Crafts Club '35; Christian Endeavor Society '34; Garden Club '32, '33, '34; G. R. Senior Club '34, '35; Glee Club '32, '34, '35; Teacher at Kalihi Union '35; Teacher at Castle Kindergarten '35. *6-8-85 aloha! Marjorie Alo Morgan*

JOSEPH K. ANAKALEA

"Hidden thoughts are lingering in his mind."

HILO, HAWAII *Joe Anakalea 1985*

ENTERED K. S. B. FROM PREPARATORY DEPARTMENT

COURSE: ELECTRICITY

Silver Pin '35; R. O. T. C. Cadet Supply Sgt. '32; Cadet Sgt. '33; C. E. Society '28, '29, '30, '31, '32, '33, '34; Class Officer, President '29, Vice President, '34; Student Council '29, '30; Kodak Club '28; Vice President '34; Pioneer Club '28; Hi-Y '30, '31, '32, '33; Junior Track '30, '31; Hobby Club '30, '35; Torch Race (winners) '33; Canteen Manager '35.

JOSEPH ANUHEA

"It isn't life that matters, 'tis the courage you bring to it."

KAPAA, KAUAI

ENTERED K. S. B. FROM KAPAA GRAMMAR SCHOOL

COURSE: WELDING

Silver Pin '30, '31, '32, '33, '34, '35; Junior Football '33, Varsity '34, '35; Inter-dorm Football '32, Basketball '32; R. O. T. C. Cadet, Corporal '33, First Sgt. '34, Cadet Captain '35; Hi-Y Club '33, '34; Secretary '33; Class Secretary and Treasurer '32, '33, '34, '35; Quill and Scroll '34, '35, President '35; Ka Moi Staff '33, '34, '35, Assistant Editor '34, '35; National Honor Society '34, '35 Student President (N. H. S.) '35; C. E. Society '33, '34, '35, Secretary '3 Canteen Manager '35.

KENNETH L. BELL *Kenny Bell* 6/8/85

"Few men are masters of things they say."

HILO, HAWAII

ENTERED K. S. B. FROM KAPIOLANI SCHOOL

COURSE: WELDING

Silver Pin '34, '35; Varsity Football '35; Junior Football '34; Track '35; C. E. Society '34; Harmony Boys Orchestra '35; Band '29, '33; Hi-Y Club '32; Pioneer Club '29; Hobby Club '29; Swimming team '34; R. O. T. C. Cadet Acting Adjutant '34; Church Member (B. M. C.) '34; Class Song Leader '35; R. O. T. C. Cadet First Lt. '35.

MARYADAMS KALIKO BURGESS

"The daintiest last, to make the end most sweet."

HONOLULU, OAHU

ENTERED K. S. G. FROM MAEMAE SCHOOL, 1930

Vice President of Class '33; R. O. T. C. Band Sponsor '35; Ka Moi Staff, Assistant Society Editor '34, Circulation Manager '35; Teacher at Kawaiahao '35; Choir '33, '34, '35; Christian Endeavor Society '31, '32, '34; Garden Club '32, '33, '34; G. R. Junior Club '31, '32; G. R. Senior Club 34, '35; Glee Club '33, '34, '35; Dancing Club '30, '31, '32, '33; Know Your City Club '31; Discussion Club '34, '35; French Club '35; Dramatic Club '30; Teacher at Castle Kindergarten; Gold Pin, Shorthand Penmanship Award, '34, '35.

LLOYD AI CHANG *Lloyd Ai Chang* 6/8/85

"Ladies call him sweet, with love enduring."

HONOLULU, OAHU

ENTERED K. S. B. FROM CENTRAL JUNIOR HIGH SCHOOL

COURSE: AUTO MECHANIC

Silver Pin '33; Track '33, '34; R. O. T. C. Cadet Corporal '33, Cadet First Lt. '35; Hi-Y '32, '33; C. E. Society '33, '34, '35; Glee Club '33, '34, '35; Explorers Club, '30; Kodak Club '32, '33, '34; Ka Moi Staff '33, '34.

BEATRIX NALEILEHUA ONAHIENAENA COCKETT

"Some are born great, some achieve greatness,
And some have greatness thrust upon them."

PAIA, MAUI

ENTERED K. S. G. FROM MAUI STANDARD SCHOOL, 1931

Silver Pin '34; Treasurer of Class '33; Ka Moi Staff '34, Proofreader '35; S. S. Teacher at Kaumakapili '35; Christian Endeavor Society '31, '32, '33, '34; Choir '34, '35; Art Crafts Club '32, '33; Garden Club '32, '33, '34; G. R. Junior Club '32, '33, Senior Club '34, 35; Glee Club 33, '34, '35; Dancing Club '32; Dramatic Club, President '31; Know Your City Club '31; Discussion Club '35; Treasurer '35; French club '35; Teacher at Castle Kindergarten '35; Health Clinic Conference '34.

FRANK COCKETT *Frank M. Cockett* 6/8/85

"His heart was light, so beauty called and glory showed the way."

WAILUKU, MAUI

ENTERED K. S. B. FROM PREPARATORY DEPARTMENT

COURSE: CARPENTRY

Varsity Football '33, '34, '35; Junior Football '32; Basketball '31, '32, '33, '34; Varsity Track '31, '32, '33, 34; Interscholastic All-Star Center 32; Inter-dorm Baseball '35; R. O. T. C. Cadet Corporal '32, Sgt. '33, First Sgt. '34, Captain '35; Hi-Y, President '32, Hi-Y Club (Kam Warriors) '30, '31, '32, '33, '34; C. E. Society '30, '31, '32, '33, '34, President 35; Glee Club '33, '34, '35; Choir '34; Class Vice President '30, '31, '32; Ka Moi Staff '33, '34, '35; Associate Member B. M. C.) '33, '34, '35; Nature Club '29; Pioneer Club '29; Boxing Team '34; Polo Club '33, '34; Interscholastic Football All-Star End '35; Interscholastic Football Championship Team '35.

VIVIAN MAILELANI COCKETT

"A rose is sweeter in the bud than full bloom."

WAILUKU, MAUI

ENTERED K. S. G. FROM MAUI STANDARD SCHOOL, 1930

Silver Pin '33, '34, '35; Class Councillor '30; Vice President of Class '31; President of Class '32; Ka Moi Staff, Assistant Recorder '34, Head Recorder '35; S. S. Teacher at K. S. G. '35; Choir '33, '34, '35; Christian Endeavor Society '30, '31, '33, President '32, '34; Garden Club '32, '33, '34; G. R. Junior Club '32, '33; G. R. Senior Club, Secretary '34, President '35; Glee Club '30, '31, '32, '33, '34, '35; Orchestra '34; Discussion Club 35; French Club '35; Harmony Club '35; Class Song Leader '30, '31, '32, '33, '34, '35; Teacher at Castle Kindergarten '35; Delegate to Kauai '34; Know Your City Club, Treasurer '31; National Honor Society '35; Quill and Scroll Society '35.

HAUNANI K. COOPER

"But who can paint like Nature? Can imagination boast, amid its gay creation, hues like hers?"

HANA, MAUI

ENTERED K. S. G. FROM HANA SCHOOL, 1931

Gold Pin '35; Silver Pin '31, '32, '33, '34, '35; National Honor Society '34, '35; Secretary of Class '31; Vice President of Class '32; Ka Moi Staff '34, '35; S. S. Teacher at St. Andrews '35; Christian Endeavor Society '31, '32, '33, '34, '35, Vice President '31; Garden Club '32, '33, '34; Glee Club '34, '35, President '32; Discussion Club '34, '35; French Club '35; Kodak Club, President '35; Dramatic Club '31; Faculty Councillor '32, '35; Vice President of Student Body '35; Delegate to Kauai; Girl Reserves '31, Vice President '32, Ring Chairman '33, President, '34, Social Chairman '35; Senior Play, "Pot Boiler" '35.

ERNEST A. DIAS

"His winning smile made him a favorite among the girls."

HONOLULU, OAHU

ENTERED K. S. B. FROM LILIUOKALANI JUNIOR HIGH SCHOOL

COURSE: AGRICULTURE

Varsity Football '34, '35; Junior Track Team '31, '32; Varsity Track Team '33, '34, '35; R. O. T. C. Cadet Corporal '33, Sgt '34, Cadet First Lt '35; Hi-Y Club '31, '32; C. E. Society '31, '34, '35; Glee Club '34, '35; Choir '33, '34; Nature Club '30, '31, 34; Gigolo Club 33; Boxing 34; Tumbling Club '34.

HERBERT DUNN

"Keep her; for she is thy life."

KAHUKU, OAHU

ENTERED K. S. B. FROM PREPARATORY DEPARTMENT

COURSE: ELECTRICITY

Silver Pin '32, '34; Junior Football '33; Varsity Football '34, '35; Basketball '32, '33, '34; Baseball '32, '33, '34, '35; R. O. T. C. Cadet Corporal '33, First Sgt. '34, Cadet First Lt. '35; Hi-Y '32, '33; C. E. Society '29, '31, '33, '34, '35; Band '29, '31, 32, 33, 34; Class Vice President 33; Class President '34, '35; Student Council '29, '32; Cine Club '29; Machine Shop Hobby '31; Pioneer Club '31; Ka Moi Staff '34, '35; Church Member (B. M. C.) '34, '35; Glee Club '34; Hui Oiwi '35; Big Six Committee '34, '35; Canteen Manager '35.

MARY KEKAHAUALANI DUVAUCHELLE

"As sweet and musical as Apollo's lute, Her voice makes heaven drowsy with the harmony."

HONOLULU, OAHU

ENTERED K. S. G. FROM SACRED HEART'S CONVENT, 1930

Silver Pin '35; Vice President of Class '30; Faculty Councillor '30, '33; President of Class '31; Class Councillor '32; Ka Moi Staff '34, Sports Editor '35; S. S. Teacher at Kalihi Union '35; Choir '33, '34, '35; Christian Endeavor Society '33, Secretary '31, Vice President '32, '34; Art Crafts Club '32; Garden Club '33, '34; G. R. Senior Club '34, Ring Chairman '35; Glee Club '30, '31, '32, '33, '34, President '35; Dancing Club '31, '32; Dramatic Club 30; Know Your City Club, Vice President '31; French Club '35; Teacher at Castle Kindergarten '35; Health Queen '33; Senior Play, "Thank You, Doctor" '35.

COMFORT EATON

"Counsel of men is like the gathering of bees."

HILO, HAWAII

ENTERED K. S. B. FROM HILO JUNIOR HIGH SCHOOL

COURSE: ELECTRICITY

Silver Pin '35; Junior Football '32; Varsity Football '33, '34, '35; Junior Basketball '32, '33; Varsity Basketball '34; R. O. T. C. Cadet Corporal '33, Sgt. '34, Cadet Major '35; Hi-Y Club '32, '33; Junior C. E. Society '31; C. E. Society '33; Swimming team '34; Boxing '35; Bix Six Committee '35.

FOLINGA FAUFATA

"His heart holds secrets of unknown thoughts."

HANA, MAUI

ENTERED K. S. B. FROM HANA GRAMMAR SCHOOL

COURSE: MARINE ENGINEERING

Varsity Football '33; Basketball '32; Hi-Y Club '32, '33; C. E. Society '31, '32, '33; Hui Oiwi Club '32, '33, '34, '35; R. O. T. C. Cadet First Sgt. '34; Cadet Captain '35.

JACOB HAILI

"Weakness is revealed by thy action of life."

WAILUKU, MAUI

ENTERED K. S. B. FROM PREPARATORY DEPARTMENT

COURSE: MACHINIST

Silver Pin '29, '30, '31; Junior Football '34, Varsity '35; Track Team '33, '34; Rifle Team '32, '33; R. O. T. C. Cadet Corporal '33, First Sgt. '34, Cadet Captain '35; Hi-Y Club '32, '33, '34, '35; Orchestra '34; Glee Club '32, '33, '34, '35; Choir '33, '34, '35; Nature Club 30; Hui Oiwi '33, '34, '35; Tumbling Club, Assistant Director '34; Gigolo Club '33, '34; Ka Moi Staff '34, '35; C. E. Society '31, '32, '33, '34, '35; Band '30, '31, '32, '33, '34, '35.

CHARLES M. HARDEE

"Bear it forever that knowledge is everywhere."

HONOLULU, OAHU

ENTERED K. S. B. FROM PREPARATORY DEPARTMENT

COURSE: MARINE ENGINEERING

Silver Pin '34, '35; Junior Football '33; Midget Basketball '31, Junior '32; Track '32, '33, '34, '35; Junior Baseball '31, Varsity '32, '33, '34, '35; R. O. T. C. Cadet Corporal '33, Cadet Sgt. '34, Cadet Major '35; Hi-Y Club '33; C. E. Society '30, '31, '32, '33, '34; Band '29, '30, '31, '32, '33, '34; Glee Club '33, '34; Choir '33; Student Council '30; Bugler '29, '30, '31, '32, '33; Kam Warriors Club '29, '30; Hobby Club '29, '35; Rifle Team '31; Ka Moi Staff '33, '34, '35, Head Proofreader '35; Tumbling Club '33; Big Six Committee '34, '35; Church Member (B. M. C.) '33, '34, '35; Quill and Scroll Society '35; Gigolo Club '33; National Honor Society '35; Manager, Championship Football Team '35.

CHARLES HUSTACE

"Think not of thyself, but that of others."

WAIMEA, KAUAI

ENTERED K. S. B. FROM WAIMEA JUNIOR HIGH SCHOOL

COURSE: MACHINIST

Silver Pin '33, '35; Junior Football '34, '35; R. O. T. C. Cadet 2nd Lt. '35; C. E. Society '33, '34, '35; Glee Club '34, '35; Choir '34; Tennis '34, '35; Ka Moi Staff '34, '35; Hobby Club Committee '35; Member (B. M. C.) '34, '35.

ALONZO F. HUTCHINSON

"Life does not matter, 'tis the way you face it."

HONOLULU, OAHU

ENTERED K. S. B. FROM PREPARATORY DEPARTMENT

COURSE: AGRICULTURE

Silver Pin '31, '32, '33, '34, '35; Junior Football '33, Varsity '34, '35; Basketball Midget Team '31, '32, Inter-dorm '33, '34, '35; Baseball '35; Rifle Team '30; R. O. T. C. Cadet Corporal '32, '33, Sgt. '34, Cadet Captain '35; C. E. Society '29, '30, '31, '32, '33; Band '29; Class President '31; Student Council '29, '30, '31; Nature Club 29; Drummer '29; Fighting Warrior '30, '31, '32, '33; Rifle Club '31, '32; Quill and Scroll Society '33, '34, '35; Ka Moi Staff '32, '33, '34, '35, Sport Editor '34, '35; Gigolo Club '33.

MAMIE KAWEHIONALANI JENSEN

"'Tis good to be merry and wise."

HONOLULU, OAHU

ENTERED K. S. G. FROM KALIHI-UKA SCHOOL, 1930

Silver Pin '35; Vice President of Class '32, Secretary '34; R. O. T. C. Sponsor, Co. C '35; Ka Moi Staff '34, Proofreader '35; S. S. Teacher at St. Andrews '35; Choir '33, '34; Christian Endeavor Society '30, '31, '32, '33; Garden Club '32, '33, '34; Art Crafts Club '32; Girl Reserves '32, Conference Delegate '32, Camp Delegate '33; Senior G. R. Club '34, '35; Glee Club '32, '33, '34; Dramatic Club '30; Dancing Club '31, '32, '33, '34, '35; Know Your City Club '31; Sewing Club '30; Secretary-Treasurer of Kodak Club '35; Teacher at Castle Kindergarten 35; Lei Day Princess '33; K. S. G. Lei Queen '35; Senior Play, "Thank You, Doctor" '35.

ELEANOR NANIALII KAINA

"No grief shall gnaw the heart,
And never shall a tender tie be broken."

HONOLULU, OAHU

ENTERED K. S. G. FROM WASHINGTON JUNIOR HIGH, 1933

S. S. Teacher at Kaumakapili '35; Christian Endeavor Society '33, '34; Garden Club '33, '34; Girl Reserves '33, '35, Camp Chairman '34; Glee Club '33, '34, '35; Ka Moi Staff '34, Proofreader '35; Dancing Club '33; Teacher at Castle Kindergarten '35.

KATHERINE KALAHUI

"If all the year were playing holidays,
To sport would be as tedious as to work."

HONOLULU, OAHU

ENTERED K. S. G. FROM McKINLEY HIGH SCHOOL, 1933

Silver Pin '35; Treasurer of Class '34; Ka Moi Staff '33, Assistant Proofreader '35; S. S. Teacher at Kaumakapili '35; Choir '34; Garden '34; Girl Reserves '34, Treasurer '35; Glee Club '33, '34, '35; Sports Let 4; Choir Part-time work at Advertiser '35; Teacher at Castle Kindergarten '35; Par5; Glee work at Pan-Pacific Inc. '35; Print Shop '34, '35; Quill and Scroll Society her at Gold Pin, Shorthand Penmanship Award '35; Clarke English Prize '35.

SAMUEL M. KAMAKAU

"My son, forget not my law."

KONA, HAWAII

ENTERED K. S. B. FROM PREPARATORY DEPARTMENT

COURSE: AGRICULTURE

Silver Pin '32; Junior Track '31, Varsity '33, '34, '35; R. O. T. C. Cadet Corporal '33, Sgt. '34; Hi-Y Club '32, '33; C. E. Society '30, '31, '32, '33, '34, '35; Glee Club '32, 33, 34; Choir 33; Kodak Club '29; Nature Club '30; Pioneer Club '30, '31; Misogynist Club '33, '34; Ka Moi Staff '33, '34, '35, Sports Editor '34, Head Copyreader '35; Member (B. M. C.) '29, '30, '31, '32, '33, '34, '35.

JOSEPH KIM

4/8/35 J Kim

"Troublesome thoughts are in narrow minds."

HUELO, MAUI

ENTERED K. S. B. FROM KOREAN CHRISTIAN INSTITUTE

COURSE: AUTO MECHANIC

Silver Pin '33, '34, '35; Junior Football '34; Track '34, '35; Baseball '33; R. O. T. C. Cadet Sgt. '34, Cadet Captain '35; Hi-Y '33, '34; C. E. Society '33, '34, '35; National Honor Society '34, '35; Ka Moi Staff '33, '34, '35; Church Member (B. M. C.) '34, '35; Captain of Inter-dorm Baseball Team '35.

MARY LUHAUPUA KAM LIN KUNANE

"Constant practice often excells even talent."

HONOLULU, OAHU

ENTERED K. S. G. FROM WAIALAE SCHOOL, 1930

Silver Pin '31, '34, '35; Quill and Scroll '35; Faculty Councillor '31; Class Secretary '33, Vice President '34, President '35; Ka Moi Staff '34, Assistant Head Copyreader '35; S. S. Teacher at St. Mary's Mission '35; Christian Endeavor Society '30, '31, '32, '33, '34; Choir '33, '34, '35; Garden Club '32, '33, '34; Girl Scouts '33, Patrol Leader '34; Color Bearer '35; Vice President of Junior Glee Club '32; Glee Club '33, '34, '35; Orchestra '34; Secretary, Know Your City Club '31; Harmony Club '35; Dramatic Club '30; Teacher at Castle Kindergarten '35; Delegate to Kokokahi Music Summer School '32, '34; Assistant Class Song Leader '35; Health Clinic Conference '34.

LEINAALA MYRA LEE

Leinaala L. Apau
6-8-85

"Silence is the perfect herald of joy; I were but little happy, if I could say how much."

HONOLULU, OAHU

ENTERED K. S. G. FROM LANAKILA SCHOOL, 1930

Silver Pin '33, '34, '35; Quill and Scroll '34, '35; Class Secretary '32; Ka Moi Staff, Head Copyreader '35; Substitute S. S. Teacher '35; Christian Endeavor Society '30, '31, '32, '33; Garden Club '32, '33, '34; Girl Reserves '31, '32, '33, '34, '35; G. R. Delegate to Kauai '34; Teacher at Castle Kindergarten '35; Glee Club '32, '33, '34, '35; Orchestra '34; Dancing Club '30, '31, '32; Dramatic Club '30; French Club '35; Health Clinic Conference '34; Ka Moi Staff '34, '35.

ELSIE MAHEALANI LONG

Elsie Long Faris

"Reading is to the mind, what exercise is to the body."

WAILUKU, MAUI

ENTERED K. S. G. FROM WAILUKU JUNIOR HIGH SCHOOL, 1932

S. S. Teacher at Kaumakapili '35; Christian Endeavor Society '34, '35; Art Crafts Club '35; Choir '34, '35; Garden Club '32, '33, '34; G. R. Senior Club '34, '35; Glee Club '32, '33, '34, '35; Ka Moi Staff '34, Proofreader '35; Dancing Club '33, '34, '35; Clarke English Prize Winner '35; Teacher at Castle Kindergarten '35; Health Clinic Conference '34.

June 8, 1935

BELLE LOUISE LEILEHUA LOWRY

"Her virtue and the conscience of her worth,
That would be woo'd and not unsought be won."

WAIOHINU, KAU, HAWAII

ENTERED K. S. G. FROM NAALEHU SCHOOL, 1932

S. S. Teacher at St. Elizabeth '35; Christian Endeavor Society '32, '33, '34, '35; Choir '34, '35; Garden Club '32, '33; Vegetable Garden Club '34; Girl Reserve '32.-'35, Senior G. R. Song Leader '34, Program Chairman '35; Glee Club '32, '33, '34, '35; Ka Moi Staff '34, Assistant Girls' School Editor '35; Football Song Leader '33, '34, '35; Discussion Club '34, '35; Teacher at Castle Kindergarten '35; Health Leader '32, '33, '35.

REBECCA KAIKAINALII MACY

"The noblest mind the best contentment has."

HONOLULU, OAHU

ENTERED K. S. G. FROM ST. ANDREW'S PRIORY, 1930

Silver Pin '30, '31, '32, '33, '34, '35; Class Secretary-Treasurer '30, Treasurer '31; Treasurer of Student Council '35; S. S. Teacher at Kawaiahao '35; Christian Endeavor Society '32, '33, '34; Art Crafts Club '32; Secretary '31; Choir '34, '35; Garden Club '32, '33, '34; Girl Reserves '32, '33; Senior G. R. Reporter '34; Service Chairman '35; Glee Club '33, '34, '35; Ka Moi Staff '34; Assistant Recorder '35; Dancing Club '31, '32; Dramatic Club '30; Vice President '31; Discussion Club '34; President '35; French Club '35; Teacher at Castle Kindergarten '35; Part-time work at Pan-Pacific '35; Print Shop '35; Quill and Scroll '35.

MADELINE AWAALIA MAHOE

"Humility, that lovely, sweet root,
From which all heavenly virtues shoot."

HONOLULU, OAHU

ENTERED K. S. G. FROM MAEMAE SCHOOL, 1930

S. S. Teacher at Kaumakapili '35; Christian Endeavor Society '32, '34; Art Crafts Club '32; Choir '34, '35; Garden Club '32, '33, '34; Senior G. R. Club '34, '35; Glee Club '33, '34, '35; Ka Moi Staff '34, Exchange Editor '35; Guitar and Ukulele Club '31; Dramatic Club '30; Teacher at Castle Kindergarten '35; Part-time work at Print Shop '35; Cheer Leader '34, '35.

SARAH LUA MAIALOHA

"For never anything can be amiss
When simpleness and duty tender it."

PAPAIKOU, HAWAII

ENTERED K. S. G. FROM HILO JUNIOR HIGH SCHOOL, 1933

S. S. Teacher at Kaumakapili '35; Christian Endeavor Society '33, '34; Choir '34, '35; Garden Club '33; Vegetable Garden '34; Girl Scouts '33, '34, '35; Glee Club '34, '35; Orchestra '33, '34; Clarke English Prize Winner '34; Teacher at Castle Kindergarten '35.

IVANHOE McGREGOR

"All the words of my mouth are in righteousness."

HONOLULU, OAHU

ENTERED K. S. B. FROM CENTRAL JUNIOR HIGH SCHOOL

COURSE: COMMERCIAL

Silver Pin '34; Varsity Baseball '35; Hi-Y Club '33; C. E. Society '32, '33; Band '32, '33, '34; Ka Moi Staff '32, '33, '34, '35, Assistant Editor '34, '35; Straight Eight Club '33; Quill and Scroll Society '33, '34, '35.

WALTER MOOKINI

"His heart holds the secrets of endeavoring thoughts."

LAHAINA, MAUI

ENTERED K. S. B. FROM PUUKOLII GRAMMAR SCHOOL

COURSE: AGRICULTURE

Silver Pin '35; Junior Football '34, Varsity '35; Basketball '33, '34, '35; Track '33; R. O. T. C. Cadet Corporal '32, Sgt. '33, Cadet First Sgt. '34, Cadet Captain '35; Hi-Y '32, '33; Glee Club '32, '33, '34, '35; Choir '33; Ka Moi Staff '33, '34 '35, Assistant Copyreader '34, Assistant Vocational Editor '35; Misogynist Club '33, '34; Nature Club '31.

JAMES L. NAKAPAAHU, JR.

"The fruit of righteousness is the foundation of life."

MAKAWELI, KAUAI

ENTERED K. S. B. FROM KALAKAUA JUNIOR HIGH SCHOOL

COURSE: MARINE ENGINEERING

Silver Pin '33, '34; Junior Football '32, '33, Varsity '33, '34, '35; Championship Football Team '35; Inter-dorm Basketball '30, '31, '32; Inter-dorm Baseball '30, '31, '32, '33, '34, 35; Junior Baseball '32, Varsity '32, '33, '34, '35; Rifle Team '32, '33, '34, '35; R. O. T. C. Cadet Corporal '32, Sgt. '33, First Sgt '34, Cadet Captain '35; Hi-Y '31, '32, '33; C. E. Society 32, '33, '34, '35; Vice President C. E. Society '35; Band '30, '31, '32, '33, '34, '35; Orchestra '30, '31, '32; Glee Club '32, '33, '34, '35; Class Vice President '35; Hobby Fair Committee '35; Quill and Scroll Society '35; Ka Moi Staff '32, '33, '34, '35, Assistant Vocational Editor '34, Editor-in-chief '35; Straight Eight Club '33; String Instrument Club '32, '33, 34; Boxing '33, '34; Kodak Club '34; Hui Oiwi '32, '33, '34, President '35; Big Six Committee '35.

GLADYS KEALOHAMINAMINA NAONE

"Her hidden silence makes many wonder."

HANA, MAUI

ENTERED K. S. G. FROM HANA SCHOOL, 1931

S. S. Teacher at St. Mary's '35; Christian Endeavor Society '31, '32, '33; Garden Club '32, '33, '34; Girl Reserve Club '31, '32, '33, '34, '35; Ka Moi Staff '34, Assistant Exchange Editor '35; French Club '35; Teacher at Castle Kindergarten '35; Class Secretary '35.

ELLEN NIOLOPA STEWART

"Genius is mainly an affair of energy."

HONOLULU, OAHU

ENTERED K. S. G. FROM ST. ANDREWS PRIORY, 1931

Silver Pin '34; Gold Pin '35; Quill and Scroll Society '34, Co-President '35; National Honor Society President '35; President of Student Council '35; Class President '33; Class Councillor '35; Ka Moi Staff, Assistant Exchange Editor '34, Girls' School Editor '35; S. S. Teacher at K. S. G. '35; Christian Endeavor Society '31, '32, '33, '35, Treasurer '34; Garden Club '32, '33, '34; Girl Scouts '34, Secretary '35; Glee Club '33, '34, '35; Teacher at Castle Kindergarten '35; Dancing Club '31; Discussion Club '34; Secretary '35; French Club '35; Health Leader '34; Health Clinic Conference '34; Class Treasurer '31; SALUTATORIAN.

LENA KAUAHILANI SUPE

"How far that little candle throws her beams! So shines a good deed in a wide world."

HILO, HAWAII

ENTERED K. S. G. FROM HILO JUNIOR HIGH SCHOOL, 1931

Silver Pin '32, '33, '34; Class Councillor '34; Class Vice President '35; Quill and Scroll '34, Secretary '35; S. S. Teacher at Kalihi Union '35; Christian Endeavor Society '31, '34, '35; Art Crafts Club '33; Garden Club '32, '33, '34; Girl Reserve Club '35; Girl Scouts '31; Ka Moi Staff, Circulation Manager '34, Editor-in-chief '35; R. O. T. C. Sponsor of Co. B '35; Stamp Club '31, '32; Dancing Club '31; Teacher at Castle Kindergarten '35.

SOON KIM TAI

"Dimples will charm, with giggles of laughter."

HANA, MAUI

ENTERED K. S. B. FROM HANA GRAMMAR SCHOOL

COURSE: AUTO MECHANIC

Silver Pin '34; Assistant Football Manager '35; Hi-Y '33, '34; C. E. Society '33, '34, '35; Glee Club '35; Ka Moi Staff '32, '33, '34, '35; R. O. T. C. Cadet Sgt. '33, '34; Cadet First Lt. '35; Hui Oiwi '35.

EDMUND VASCONCELLOS

"Music in his fingers is like rythm in his speech."

PAIA, MAUI

ENTERED K. S. B. FROM ST. ANTHONY SCHOOL

COURSE: COMMERCIAL

Junior Football '35; Inter-dorm Baseball '33, '34, '35; Football '33, '34, '35; Varsity Track '34, '35; Varsity Baseball '35; R. O. T. C. Cadet Corporal '33, Sgt. '34, Cadet Second Lt. '35; Hi-Y '33, '34; Ka Moi Staff '34, '35; Boxing Club '34, '35; Tennis '34, '35, Champion '34, 35.

HENRY WATSON

"The sound of music enlightens my heart."

HUELO, MAUI

ENTERED K. S. B. FROM MAUI HIGH SCHOOL

COURSE: MACHINIST

Junior Football 32, Varsity '33, '34, '35; Track '33, '34, '35; R. O. T. C. Cadet Color Sgt. '33, Sgt '34, Cadet Second Lt. '35; Hi-Y Club '32, '33, '34; C. E. Society '30, '31, '32, '33; Glee Club '31, '32, '33, '34, '35; Choir '33, '34; Straight Eight Club '33; Ka Moi Staff '33, '34; String Instrument '32, '33, '34; Tennis '35; Championship Football Team, Co C '32; Church Member (B. M. C.) '34, '35; Senior Play, "Thank You, Doctor" '35.

GEORGE N. WEST

"'Tis better to be a crystal and be broken than to be a tile on the roof top"

HILO, HAWAII

ENTERED K. S. B. FROM PREPARATORY DEPARTMENT

COURSE: COMMERCIAL

Silver Pin '31, '34, '35; Inter-dorm Football '34, '35, Baseball '32, '33; R. O. T. C. Cadet Coproral '33, Sgt. '34, Cadet First Lt. '35; National Honor Society '34; '35; Hi-Y '33; C. E. Society '30, '31, '32, '33, '34; Band '30, '31; Discussion Club Secretary '34; Kodak Club '34, '35; President, '34; Quill and Scroll Society '34, '35; Bugler '31, '32, '33; Ka Moi Staff 32, '33, '34, '35, Head Proofreader '34, Circulation Staff '33, Assistant Editor '35; Hobby Club Committee '35; Printing Club '31; Yell Leader '33, '34, '35; Big Six Committee '35; National Oratorical Contest '33; Alumni Oratorical Contest '34, '35; Clarke English Prize Winner '34, '35; Dramatic Club '32; Tumbling Club '33; Athletic Letter Pin '35; Senior Play "The Pot Boiler" '35; VALEDICTORIAN.

ELMER W. WILLIAMSON

"Concentrating mind increases thy knowledge of learning."

MAKAWAO, MAUI

ENTERED K. S. B. FROM PREPARATORY DEPARTMENT

COURSE: CARPENTRY

Silver Pin '34, '35; Inter-dorm Football '33, '34, '35; Junior Track '31, Varsity '33, '35; Hi-Y Club '32, '34, '35; C. E. Society '30, '31, '32, '33, '34, '35; Vice President Three Musketeers Club '33; Kodak Club '29, '30, '31, '32; R. O. T. C. Cadet Second Lt. '35; Church Member (B. M. C.) '35; Hobby Fair Committee '29, '30, '31, '35; Boxing Club '34, '35; Baseball '34, '35; Basketball '33, '34, '35.

VIRGINIA PENALIILII WO

'Grace was in all her steps, heaven in her eyes,
In every gesture dignity and love."

WAIOHINU, KAU, HAWAII

ENTERED K. S. G. FROM NAALEHU SCHOOL, 1932

Silver Pin '32, '33, '34, '35; National Honor Society '35; Quill and Scroll Society '35; S. S. School Teacher at Kalihi Union '35; Class Councillor '33; Class President '34; Class Treasurer '35; Art Crafts Club '32; Choir '33, '34, '35; Garden Club '32, '33, '34; Girl Scouts '32-'35, Treasurer '34, '35, Patrol Leader '34, Lieutenant '35; Glee Club '33,' 34' ,35; Ka Moi Staff '34, Proofreader '35; Teacher at Castle Kindergarten '35; Part-time work at Print Shop '34, '35; Part-time work at Pan-Pacific '35.

EVELYN KEOHOKAPULANI YATES

"Nothing is great but the inexhaustible wealth of Nature."

KEALAKEKUA, HAWAII

ENTERED K. S. G. FROM KONAWAENA SCHOOL, 1930

Silver Pin '34; Christian Endeavor Society '31, '32, '33, '34, '35; S. S. Teacher at St. Elizatbeth '35; Garden Club '32, '33, '34; Girl Scouts 34, '35, Treasurer '35; Glee Club '32, '33, '34, Librarian '35, Ka Moi Staff '34; Society Editor '35; Dancing Club '30, '31, '32; Dramatic Club '30; Teacher at Castle Kindergarten '35; Part-time work at Advertiser '35.

JAMES YIM

"To receive instruction is wise dealing."

HONOLULU, OAHU

ENTERED K. S. B. FROM KALAKAUA JUNIOR HIGH SCHOOL

COURSE: ELECTRICITY

Silver Pin '32; Inter-dorm Baseball '33, '34, '35, Football '33, '34, '35; Hi-Y Club '32, '33; R. O. T. C. Cadet Sgt. '34, Cadet Second Lt. '35; Ka Moi Staff '34; Rifle Club '34.

WILLIAM YOMES

"His talented hands contain much success in music."

HONOLULU, OAHU

ENTERED K. S. B. FROM KALAKAUA JUNIOR HIGH

COURSE: MACHINIST

Silver Pin '34; Junior Football '34, Varsity '35; Track '33, '34; R. O. T. C. Cadet Corporal '33; C. E. Society '33, '34, '35; Hi-Y '33, '34; Glee Club '34, '35; Orchestra '34, '35; String Instrument Club '33, '34, '35.

GIRLS' CLASS HISTORY

We, the members of the class of '35, seeing that the time for our departure from Kamehameha is approaching, and having reached the higher attainments Kamehameha can offer, wish to make others realize that we will always feel love, affection, and loyalty for our alma mater in which we spent six brief, but happy years.

Anyone familiar with Kamehameha could tell of remarkable changes from the shy and insignificant seventh graders to the present dignified seniors.

First, in 1929 as small sisters, bewildered, frightened and yet excited at being a part of Kamehameha, we, the original twelve girls of the class of '35 adapted ourselves gradually to our Kamehameha home. We entered into the social circle having our first class picnic at Hanauma Bay, and received Honorable mention in the annual song contest. Thus concluded our seventh grade year with new friends and new experiences.

We returned in the fall of 1930-31 enthusiastic and eager with new additions to our little family. We became the proud possessors of the Mary A. Richards' cup obtained from the annual song contest. Though a few difficulties came our way, our eighth grade year came to a close with better prospects for a more successful coming year.

The third year in Kamehameha made us real "freshies" enthralled over our new environment situated high near the mountain tops of Kapalama Heights where we attempted to sought for higher and better things. There was our class picnic at Kailua, our winning the Mary A. Richards' cup for the second consecutive year, our capturing first prize for the Health Week Yell contest, our first freshmen function, a never-to-be-forgotten affair, and there came the privilege of receiving callers in the gymnasium. This was in 1932-33.

From lofty "freshies," the fall of '33 brought us down to mere sophomores. Among the outstanding features of our tenth grade year were our annual class picnic at Kailua, and the sponsoring of the Health Week held annually by each tenth grade Home-Hygiene class. The year proved enjoyable for the "suffering" sophomores.

As gleeful juniors we came back with a determination to strive and work harder for we were upper classmen. We proved that we possessed talent in music and dancing by singing and performing at the Waialua Theatre. Our junior class dance will be remembered as one with much gaiety. Two of our outstanding students, Ellen Stewart and Virginia Wo, represented our class in the Alumni Oratorical contest. We were the first class to work at the various Health Clinics in the different vicinities of Honolulu. The promenade we gave for the seniors, at the "Cherry Blossom Garden," will forever bring back memories of a real junior-senior prom.

Our last stretch of progress and achievement came during our last year in school— our senior year. We were determined to work still harder, not only to be graduates of our school, but to obtain success in our undertakings in the future. "Lei Day Memories," a musical presentation will always stand out as a successful student program. For the first time during our senior high school days, we placed first in the annual song contest and received the New England Mother's cup. We became the managers of the Senior Practice Cottage, and cared for "Baby Dana." Not only were we Sunday School teachers, but also cadets at the Castle Kindergarten. In athletics we became volleyball and basketball champs. The privilege of a Tuesday afternoon out was granted us. Members of our class are represented in both the National Honor and Quill and Scroll Societies. The John Clarke awards for improvement in English went to Elsie Long and Katherine Kalahui. In scholastic achievement we boast two gold pin students. In the social way, we have been fortunate in being entertained at a luau given by Miss Maude E. Schaeffer and Dr. Homer F. Barnes, and at a tea by Miss Winifred Wing. And then there was the junior-senior promenade! Thus concluded our senior year of work and play.

Miss Marguerite Judson, our senior class adviser, has stood by us faithfully during our last year in Kamehameha, guiding us through difficulties, encouraging us when we needed it, sharing our joys in work and play and ever urging us toward our goal.

How can we attempt to say farewell to our alma mater? There is both anticipation and regret as we leave Kamehameha.

Though there are memories surrounding those who have been our teachers and friends, we cannot remain with them always for we must sample further experiences in life. After all, commencement is just the beginning for us, but we shall always cherish the thoughts of our days in Kamehameha.

GIRLS' POPULARITY CONTEST

Prettiest	Mary Duvauchelle
Daintiest	Mamie Jensen
Tallest	Mele Ainoa
Shortest	Evelyn Yates
Most Mysterious	Beatrice Cockett
Most Musical	Mary Kunane
Most Dramatic	Marjorie Alo
Class Orator	Ellen Stewart
Busiest	Virginia Wo
Wittiest	Maile Cockett
Peppiest	Belle Lowry
Most Dependable	Gladys Naone
Best All-Round Athlete	Katherine Kalahui
Most Fastidious	Kaliko Burgess
Luckiest	Sarah Maialoha
Most Ambitious	Haunani Cooper
Noisiest	Eleanor Kaina
Most Romantic	Irene Akeo
Most Kiddish	Lena Supe
Slimmest	Leinaala Lee
Most Original	Elsie Long
Friendliest	Madeline Mahoe
Best Natured	Rebecca Macy

MISS MAUDE E. SCHAEFFER
Principal of Kamehameha School for Girls.

BOYS' CLASS HISTORY

The twenty-five members of the Class of Nineteen Hundred and Thirty-five bid our friends, the faculty and students of the Kamehameha Schools—ALOHA.

We have passed the twelfth milestone of our high school education, and we are now endeavoring to take the opportunities that have been bestowed upon us and bear our learned facilities of knowledge through life which is before us.

The following nine members, Alonzo Hutchinson, George West, Herbert Dunn, Frank Cockett, Charles Hardee, Joseph Anakalea, Elmer Williamson, Jacob Haili and Samuel Kamakau, were pupils of the Preparatory school under the leadership of the late Miss Maude E. Post. We used to wear short blue serge trousers, and long black stockings, and starched shirts on holidays. We were eager to go up to the Manual department where we could drill and take part in athletic contests. We wish to express our appreciation to the faculty of the Preparatory school for what they taught us during those early days.

In our last junior high school year in 1930 we won the song contest in the junior division. We also won the senior division song contest for three consecutive year, L-11, H-11, and 12th grade years.

We wish to thank Mr. Joseph M. Kamakau for his keen interest and untiring efforts in leading us to our victories in the song contest. He has faithfully helped us for five years in the song contests, and we, in return, won four out of those five years.

We also won the annual torch race held on the school campus during our L-11th year.

Our class members have attained honors in many organizations. In the National Honor Society we are represented by Joseph Anuhea, George West and Joseph Kim, and in the Quill and Scroll we have Joseph Anuhea, George West, Charles Hardee, Alonzo Hutchinson, Ivanhoe McGregor and James Nakapaahu.

George West represented Kamehameha in the National Oratorical contest and he took part in the Alumni Oratorical contest during his H-11th and Senior years. He won the annual spelling contest in 1933

and in 1934. He has also been a yell leader for three years.

On the Big Six Committee, which is one of the big factors in the school for boys, we have Charles Hardee, Comfort Eaton, Herbert Dunn, James Nakapaahu and George West.

For recreation during our years in school we had three class picnics at Kailua; a "depression" dance during our sophomore year; and a chicken hekka dinner at the Senior practice cottage and a class picnic at Kahala while Seniors.

We were represented on the mainland by the president of our class, Herbert Dunn, who spent his Christmas vacation with his uncle in Los Angeles.

We have contributed to this school's athletic victories in various sports under the watchful eyes of Coach William Wise. Herbert Dunn, Comfort Eaton, Joseph Anuhea, Frank Cockett earned their letters in football and also a medal for the Interscholastic Football Championship in 1934. Henry Watson, Kenneth Bell, Walter Mookini, Jacob Haili, Ernest Dias, William Yomes, Folinga Faufata and Joseph Kim also did their share on the gridiron during their Junior and Senior years.

In track we have Edmund Vasconcellos, Ernest Dias, Samuel Kamakau, Frank Cockett, Charles Hardee, Elmer Williamson, Lloyd Chang, Jacob Haili, Joseph Anakalea. On the baseball diamond we have Herbert Dunn, Joseph Kim, Charles Hardee, and James Nakapaahu.

And in "range 500" we have James Nakapaahu in target practice, the dead shot of our class.

In tennis we have Frank Cockett and Walter Mookini, champions in their ninth grade year. In his sophomore year, Edmund Vasconcellos was also a champ. Charles Hustace and Henry Watson followed along in this line.

In basketball we have Frank Cockett, who was for three years on the Junior Interscholastic All-Star basketball, and Comfort Eaton, Walter Mookini, Alonzo Hutchinson and Herbert Dunn as veterans.

The Class of 1935 was noted for its splendid spirit of co-operation. The class members worked together in their support

of school projects and class enterprises. For the last five years the largest annual contribution to the Welfare Drive came from the Class of '35.

Mr. Don Mitchell joined this group in 1929 as a club leader and for the next five years acted as class advisor.

We wish to thank him for his efforts and patience and the things he did for us.

With memories of our days spent in this Alma Mater deeply imprinted on our hearts we regret leaving our friends and fellow students. Our hearts are heavy as we think of the day when we must leave our faithful institution.

The melodious notes of "Taps" will no longer be heard by the Class of '35.

MY AUTOBIOGRAPHY
Dana Marilyn Kaluna, Senior Cottage Baby

On my eleventh week birthday (and I remember I weighed twelve pounds), Mother and I rode up to the Kapalama Heights to a place where I saw large beautiful buildings. I soon learned that this was the Kamehameha School for Girls.

Upon our arrival at Senior Practice Cottage, we were greeted by a teacher and several girls who laughed at me because of my hair sticking straight up. One of the girls took my basket of clothes and led us into a room. I concluded that this must be my nursery for I saw a baby's bed, a buggy, a high chair and toys and it seemed that I was to have permanent residence here.

Miss Neva Hirleman, director of Senior Practice Cottage, was my new mother. My real mother kissed me good-bye and I heard her tell the girls to remember that I was only a borrowed baby. I, thus, entered upon my first year at the girls' boarding school.

I am sure that there is no baby who has had as many mothers as I have had—and good mothers, too! They have prepared my food and fed me, done my laundry, cleaned my nursery, kept me comfortable and even had time to play with me.

I was allowed to go home for Christmas vacation to spend the holidays with Mother and Daddy. I had much fun playing with my two brothers. After Christmas I came back fatter and wearing a blue hair ribbon. I had also learned to creep and felt very much grown-up-like.

One day as I was in my buggy on the lanai, my mother came out and saw me standing up straight alone for the first time. I guess I surprised her because every time before this when she had wanted me to stand, I would fold my legs under me. This was my red letter day because I also learned to hold my bottle. Two days later I took my first step with help. My mothers thought that I was a fine baby and had great possibilities. And of course, I have!

Now that I am grown up, I sit at the table in my high chair while my mothers eat. Sometimes they let me entertain myself by letting me watch them prepare the meals in the kitchen.

In spite of the fact that I am the smallest member of our family of seven at Senior Cottage, I am the most important. We have many guests visiting Senior Cottage and I am always the center of attraction. (I really am not conceited!)

The sad time has come when I must leave to go home. I am very thankful to my mothers for the patient care and love which they have bestowed upon me. It is my wish that I,, too, someday may become a student and live in Senior Cottage, practicing home-making and care of babies. I shall always cherish fond memories of this year.

Scottie!!!?

Terlie-Sweetie.

Taffy

Bumpy!!!!!

Flash

Bouncer!!!?

Bissaiya.

GIRLS' CLASS PROPHECY
(With apologies to Shakespeare's "Macbeth.")

Scene—The Ironwood grove on Kapalama Heights.
Three Witches are gathered around a cauldron.
There are occasional flashes of lightning and
the sound of distant thunder. It is dark except
for the fire burning under the cauldron.

Witches
Hear! O hear! O hear again!
In thunder lightning and in rain.

Fair is foul and foul is fair
Dispute our prophecies if you dare!

For we are powerful witches three
And can tell you what you will be.

Hark! We hear the voice of one
Who comes to seek us all in fun.
(Maile Cockett enters and addresses the witches.)

Maile Cockett
There is much I want to know
Tell me how the future'll go.

'Ere the hour grow too late
Every girl must know her fate.

Every senior at Kam School
Wants to hear she'll be no fool!

Witches
(Building up the fire under the cauldron)
We will tell you what you'd know
But first into the cauldron throw

The wish bone of the "hekka" chicken.
That will make our mixture thicken.

Mix in well the senior noise
And their fondness for the boys.

Throw in now some words you've learned
"Fastidious" will not be spurned;

And the money from the senior canteen
Then we can tell you what we've seen.

Melt the cup from the contest of song
Then our mixture will boil ere long.

Add all the senior things you do
To make our prophecies come true.
(Maile Cockett throws all the required ingredients
in the cauldron)

Witches
Now about the cauldron sing
With the witches in a ring.
(All dance three times around cauldron)

1st Witch
Now 'tis done—the answer lies
In this pot before our eyes.

Maile
O tell me! tell me what you see
Before time comes for me to flee!

2nd Witch
(Stirring the cauldron)
Listen now and we'll relate
What shall be the seniors fate.

Ellen Stewart wears a judge's robe;
Cases in court she tries to probe.

An opera singer is Evelyn Yates
And Kona nightingale rivals hate.

Sarah Maialoha shows great propriety
As an army woman in high society.

Lena Supe in the dancing follies
Kaneohe inmates cheers and jollies.

Going native in Samoa is Margie Alo
Why she does it—I don't know.

Mamie Jensen's dancing days are done,
In a Danish convent she's become a nun.

Give "Reporter" Belle Lowry just a hint
It will be in the news—as fit to print!
(Witches stir cauldron once again)

3rd Witch
Haunani Cooper I seem to see
At Hana U.—with her Ph. D.

Eleanor Kaina at Sing Sing "College"
Is teaching the "pupils" the talking
knowledge.

Who's the emaciated matron at K. S. G.?
Mele Ainoa! Can it really be?

Mary Kunane is covered with leis
Her piano concert has won great praise.

Irene Akeo is Uncle——wife.
She's making him happy the rest of his
life.

I see in New York a fashion shoppe,
K. Burgess, B. Cockett are the names
on top.

Their customers crowd to the very door
When R. Macy's rhumba has the floor.

(Witches dance around the cauldron again then say together)

Fair is foul and foul is fair
List to the prophecy and have a care!

1st Witch

Despite her jokes and her perversity
We see Leinaala Lee at the University.

When there's any "speeching" to be done
Katherine Kalahui will be the one.

Elsie Long, an instructor of Art,
"Alimihi" painting she loves to impart.

Gladys Naone's charm and grace
Makes home seem like the only place.

Madeline Mahoe--taxi driver of fame--
To drive Kam couples is her aim.

Mary Duvauchelle's lovely voice
At the Metropolitan opera is first choice.

A prosperous laundry—run by Virgie Wo
No credit allowed! Pay as you go!

Maile Cockett

To many—you're known for your visit
For all occassions you have a joke to fit.

Witches

The prophecy is at an end
And you away we now must send.

Maile Cockett

Will these things come really true?
Is this what the seniors are going to do?

Witches

(Brandish broomsticks at Maile)

Nearly gone is now the fire,
Not another thing inquire.
But—
Fair is foul and foul is fair,
Dispute this prophecy if you dare.

(Witches vanish)

AS WE REMEMBER HER

The first recollection we have of her is in that little old library. There have we seen her often among the books that she  loved so well. We see her lovely smile, her kindly eyes, her busy hands as she told us what books were good to read.

Our second recollection of her is in the English classroom where we began our "growing up" lessons in English. How patient she was in guiding and teaching us during our last year at the old school.

Miss Winslow

The years have gone by swiftly. Again we think of her—not in the quaint old library but in an attractive new one. We see her as day after day she used to arrange compositions and pictures on the library bulletin board.

And at the new school she again instructed us in English. She was always helping someone.

But she has departed never to return except on occasional visits. We do not see her on the campus, in Kinau Hale, or in all the familiar places.

But we have not forgotten her. We think of her still as one very dear to us.

The Class of 1935 wish to express their gratitude and aloha to their teacher and friend—MISS EMMA WINSLOW.

INFORMAL GLIMPSES

MAC

JOSIE

BAL

HAWKSHAW

TRACKSTERS

1935

GOING EAST

~HOLD-ON~

? Hungry ?

Aboriginies

Misogynist

BOYS' CLASS PROPHECY

Time: In the morning about 11 o'clock. 1950.

Place: Kona, Island of Hawaii.

Perched on a memorial stone sat two human-beings. The attention of one was focussed upon the scenery before him. The scene before this person was a towering mountain, at the top of which could be seen half of the sun. The half that could not be seen was hidden by the mountain-top and the other half was radiating gloriously. The second person looked disheartedly at all the lava rocks about them, which covered a distance of about half a mile around. Suddenly a swanky stream-lined truck passed these two persons. On the door of the truck were printed the words, MISOGYNIST COFFEE COMPANY OF SOUTHERN KONA. The two men looked at each other. Back at the car they glanced. Then recognizing the face of the driver their faces gleamed and they exclaimed, "Well, strike us pink! If it isn't Samuel Kamakau." Reassuring the assertions of the two, Sammy jumped out of the car and said, "For heaven's sake, George West and Elmer Williamson! What are you two doing here? Gosh, this is a surprise!"

"We've been shipwrecked," said Elmer. "Our sloop, the Glad Rags, burned and sank last night about a mile offshore. We swam to shore and we're lucky to be alive. We didn't know where we were but now that you've come along, it's Kona I guess."

"Yes, to be sure," replied Sammy, "you're right on the spot where the village of Hoopuloa used to be. It was wiped out by the lava flow of 1926."

"You two are certainly vagabonds, aren't you?" continued Sammy, "I know just what you two need now, come on, hop on, we're going to Hilo."

"Gee, Sammy! the way you name your company tells me you're still unmarried," remarked George. "Gosh, you're true to the bone. A Misogynist I guess you'll always be."

Sammy smiled; there was no retort. But after that smile Sammy's face changed colors. That sudden expression of his face was incomprehensible but nevertheless the conversation went on.

"Did you two finish college?" asked Sam as he stuck his head out of the window of the truck to feel the velocity of the wind.

"Yes, we did," answered George, "But after college we got the wander-lust and so we've been roaming ever since. In New York we met Charlie Hustace. He's a dancing instructor there and has his own school. Girls, boy! he has flocks of them every day. We wondered why he left the mechanical trades and he told us that he couldn't resist the beat of dancing feet.

"In Kentucky we met Joe Dias' son. You know, Ernest Dias. He graduated from the University of Kentucky. He has always wanted to be a sugar technologist. But there isn't cane in Kentucky and so he's the big butter man of that region.

"I don't have to tell you about Henry Watson. You see him in the moving pictures today. Yes, he's crooning his way through Hollywood.

"You'll be surprised to know that Charlie Hardee is making good in China. He was always interested in marine engineering and so today he owns a firm that is trying to sell engines to all the junks of the Wangze River.

"Joe Anuhea and Herbert Dunn are inseparables. We've been to New York several times. The last time we were there we met Joe and Herbert in the Radio City. Henry Afong had heard of their good work at the local plantations so he invited them over to the City. Henry is a big shot in the television field and he gave Herbert a job along that line. He made Joe superintendent of a huge steel structure that is still in the making and which will, when completed, house all of Henry's discoveries of television.

"Speaking of television that reminds us. One night while in San Francisco we heard a television program from Honolulu. Speaking fluently and without stuttering, to our surprise came the vision and voice of Edward "Tickie" Vasconcellos. He had become a politician and an accomplished orator. He was during this program reviewing the struggle that he and his partner Ivanhoe "Big-Blast" McGregor had gone through to bring to Hawaii the long desired statehood.

"After leaving the coast we sailed to

Samoa. On one of the big ocean liners that make Samoa one of its stopping place was Chief Engineer Folinga Faufata. Folinga's ship also traveled to New Zealand. Folinga told how he had strangely met Alonzo Hutchinson. He said Alonzo had changed immensely in all his features. Alonzo had become mystic, and although an eccentric old man, he was a distinguished horticulturist of New Zealand. Alonzo had a weakness for ornamental plants and it was here in New Zealand that his passion was satisfied."

Sam interrupted the s p e a k e r here. "Speaking of horticulture," he said, "you might be interested to know that Walter Mookini has a wonderful farm of vegetables on Maui. He has prospered selling lettuce, celery, sweet potatoes, beets, and all those things. He owns the greatest vegetable producing company in the islands. Miss Van Auken used to buy from him."

"I might also add," said Sam, "that Kenneth Bell is a physical director at Mountain View school. We shall see him on our way to Hilo."

"I'm sure that you two agree that Joe Anakalea was a boy of perseverance during his school days," Sam went on, "well, today he's head of the electrical department of Ewa Plantation Co. and is also a loving father. Dr. Barnes told me this in a letter."

Then the vagabonds went on with their story. Elmer told about the time he met James Nakapaahu in Idaho. James was penniless and his spirit broken down. He had joined Buck Lai Tin's baseball group that toured the mainland. But the group failed to be an attraction and hence James was just another southpaw out of a job. But today you know well that his case has been reversed. He made a comeback and he's managing the New York Giants now.

Bill Yomes was corresponding with Nakapaahu all the while. The poor old fellow had been trying to leave "bottoms-up" alone and save enough money to join James' outfit. But instead he became the popular pianist of "Tin Can Alley." At any rate he finally got a hold of himself and saved enough to sail away and become Nakapaahu's assistant manager.

As for Jim Yim you know what happened to him as well as I. He "went and done got" married on the night of our graduation. However, marriage has done wonders to him. I heard that now he sits up late at nights studying ways and means of electricity.

"I received a letter from Frank Cockett about a year ago," continued Elmer. "Frank has also been married. Lena, of course. He is a carpenter by trade. He's been building honeymoon cottages for years but he can't build one for Lena."

Frank also told me that Joseph Kim had been married too. Yes, Mamie. Soon Kim Tai still hangs around the pal of his high school days. They both, Joe and Soon, own a service station. They run their business on strictly cash terms. "Pal or no pal," wrote Frank, "charge the book is out of question with them."

"What happened to Lloyd Chang?" Sam again interrupted.

"We don't know, we haven't heard of him," said the two vagabonds simultaneously.

"Oh well," continued Sam, "you know how he was during his high school days, Detective "Hawkshaw" Chang, here now and gone the next minute."

"And what about Comfort Eaton," asked George.

"He's a rat exterminator in Hilo," answered Sam.

"He once had a job exterminating termites, bugs, insects and so forth with the Bishop Estate. He sort of became interested in that line and made it his hobby. Today he has commercialized his hobby and you'll find his office down at the wharf. Wharf rats are in his line, too."

Finally the streamlined truck reached Mountain View school where Ken Bell is stationed. "Big Body" Bell knew by heart the schedule of Sam's truck and he came running out singing at the top of his voice, "Hello there, Sam, how's the pretty maid of Kona? Have you decided on the date yet?"

"Sh-sh-sh, not so loud," said Sammy.

"So you've been holding out on us, eh?" cried Elmer, "no wonder you blushed when we called you a misogynist true to the bone. Misogynist, my eye! Come on, spill the beans, when's the date?"

"Saturday night, June 1. Jacob Haili and his syncopators will play the wedding march," said Sam giving in.

GIRLS' CLASS WILL

HEAR YE! HEAR YE! You who have come to listen to the hearing of this testament in the witnessing presence of one and all, that we, the seniors of the class of 1935 of the Kamehameha School for Girls being of a sane and sober state of mind, do hereby create and ordain this document to be our Last Will and Testimony for those who come after us, thereby bequeathing our more or less varied treasured possessions to those who, by direct hereditary rights, friendship, and habits acquired in school, are sole heirs.

As a class we bequeath the following:

First—To Miss Maude E. Schaeffer and members of the faculty we say Aloha Nui Loa with intermingling tears as we remember their kind efforts in helping to prepare our future.

Second—To our adviser, Miss Marguerite Judson, may we extend our deepest aloha and gratitude for her sincere guidance and help during our last high school year.

Third—To Miss Nelle Word, our house mother of Kinau Hale, we bequeath our greatest appreciation of her untiring efforts in trying to keep those dignified seniors quiet.

Fourth—To our Senior Cottage "mom," Miss Neva Hirleman, we bestow our many thanks of appreciation for helping prepare us to be future housewives of Hawaii Nei.

Fifth—To our Baby Dana Kaluna, we wish all the luck, success and happiness for her future.

Sixth—To those who fill our vacancies next year, we bequeath our many senior privileges plus our nine weeks home; our Sundays, Tuesdays and Thursdays teaching kiddies, and our very tempting Senior Canteen. We also bestow upon you all the fun and great deal of hard work accompanied by few tears and many smiles with the best wishes of a Mighty Senior.

Seventh—To you! O prospective Juniors, we leave our first year rooms in Kinau Hale and all the fun and punishments for Jolly Juniors.

Eighth—Suffering Sophs! What more could you expect! May your senior high school days be filled with work, Happiness, and success.

Ninth—To our little sisters who will some day follow their big sisters, we will our Saturday calling nights, our love to make noise whenever possible, and our desires to fill our stomachs at Senior Cottage. "Remember girls! don't go above the budget."

Tenth—As individuals we will the following:

Her antique freckly freckles Mele Ainoa leaves to Loretta Ainoa, and to Margaret "Small Kid" Dunn she leaves her amazing height of—oh! I can't count the number of feet.

To Alice Chang, Irene Akeo wills her Fort Street "hangout" every Saturday; to Sheba Cathcart she bequeaths her plans for the future, and to Elizabeth Stewart she leaves her frequent telephone calls from hm—!

Marjorie Alo wills her hilarious laughter and delirious moments to none other than the rightful heir, Lily "Birdie" Wilson. Keep up the record "Birdie."

To her little sister Carol Baker, Kaliko Burgess wills her basso voice, and to Ruth Burgess she leaves her rare ability to be a good little girl. Uphold the Burgess conduct, Ruth!

Beatrice Cockett wills her unusual daintiness to that tom boyish "Scotty" Vasconcellos, and to Juanita Wong her genuine ability in staring at the opposite sex.

Her genuine art of telling fish stories, Maile Cockett leaves to her little sister Elizabeth Ernst, and to Eunice Cockett, Marjorie Kunewa and Phoebe Cockett she wills her favorite expression "Maui No Ka Oe."

To Winifred Cheong, Haunani Cooper wills her leadership, and to Mary Louise Cobb-Adams, she leaves her capacity of rare artistic abilities.

To her sister Anna, Mary Duvauchelle wills her natural waves; to her little sister Bernice Campbell, she bequeaths her modest ways, and to Georgiana Bishaw she leaves her coloratura pitch. Don't give the birds competition, "Georgie."

As sponsor of Company C, Mamie Jensen leaves this honor to Lilinoe Wilson; to Allane Paris she wills her feminine ways, and to Emelia Akeo she bequeaths her technique in "tickling the uke."

To her little sister Nohea Kalaluhi, Eleanor Kaina leaves her Jean Harlow figure; to Hilda Mattson she wills her rare ability to dance, and to Cornelia Kamakau she bequeaths her nick-name C. P. W. Take heed one and all!

To her little sister Charlotte Supe, Katherine Kalahui leaves her girlish school-day figure, and to her sister Margaret, she gives her ability as an exceptional athlete.

To none other than "Anna May Wong" Aiona, Mary Kunane wills her authentic piano playing, and to her little sister Frances Nohoikaiu, she leaves her amazing relations with the opposite sex. Tut! Tut! Frances.

Her teasing ways Leinaala Lee leaves to Evelyn Rabideau; to her sister Leilani she wills her forehead slaps with those certain malemen, and to Muriel Swift her untiring efforts to count headlines on Monday nights.

Because she does not know what else to will, Elsie Long bequeaths her brain box, minus the brains, plus her thoughts, minus the thinking, to Abigail Bode, and to Lydia Afat she leaves her hope of becoming Head Nurse of the Kaneohe Hospital.

To the sole heir, Mikahala White, Belle Lowry wills her thrills with louses (really lice), and to her big, little sister Wilma Barringer, she leaves her ambition to become Physical Ed. director of the nations at the college of Timbuktu.

To Mabel Heu, Rebecca Macy bequeaths her qualifications to fullfil the position of Secretary to Governor Joseph Dwight of Nanakuli, and to her sister Emma, she leaves her silver pin record. Uphold the family honor, Emma!

Madeline Mahoe wills to Cousin Eula Benham her nick-name "Bouncer," and to her little sister Pauline Duvauchelle her unusual figure of Mae West's curves.

To her little sister Flora Salm, Sarah Maialoha leaves her frequent and enjoyable strolls through Kapiolani Park, and to Gertrude Williamson she wills her posture.

Gladys Naone gives her Hamoa Bay waves to Wynona Kaiama with the best wishes that they will help her pass her annual swimming test at K. S. G., and to Elizabeth Haia she wills her most extraordinary squeals.

To her little sister Pauline Mookini, Ellen Stewart leaves her ability to control the wheel of the student affairs, to Hermine Dreier she wills her gold pin, and her pleasant smile and slight boyishness to Leilani Allen.

To Dorothy Goo, Lena Supe wills her sponsorship, and to Frances Weir she leaves her position on the Ka Moi Staff. Go to it girls! To her sisters Juanita and Charlotte she wills her ability to enjoy her vacations, and to Loretta Ainoa she bequeaths her crazy moments.

Virginia Wo leaves her laughing childish eyes to her little sister Eleanor Fountain, and to Mina Baker her Girl Scout leadership.

Evelyn Yates wills her technique in hockey to Catherine Sims and to her small sister, Thelma Haia, she leaves her alluring ways to captivate those of the opposite sex.

TO ALL WHO GLANCE AT THIS DOCUMENT—

We hereby nominate and appoint Miss Marguerite Judson as Chief Justice of this our Last Will and Testimony without stocks or bonds.

MARGUERITE JUDSON.

In witness whereof, I hereby seal this Testament the first day of the second month of the one thousand nine hundred and thirty-fifth year of our Lord.

ELLEN STEWART.

SENIOR ACTIVITIES

CANDY CONSUMERS

STUDIOUS MEN

BUSINESS MEN

MAKING HAY WHILE ?

LIFE IN THE RAW ! FLOOD RELIEF SQUAD !

BOYS' CLASS WILL

We, the Seniors of the Kamehameha School for Boys, being of sound mind and body, do hereby make and declare public on this eighth day of March, in the year of nineteen hundred and thirty-five of our calendar, this our last will and testament; and hereby, annulling and declaring void any will or wills heretofore. made by us jointly or otherwise.

As a class, we hereby leave and extend our appreciation and sincere aloha to the administration and faculty of the Kamehameha School for Boys for their tireless efforts in preparing us to face the problems of life.

To Miss Margaret Auman and Miss Neva Hirleman, our home economic instructors, we leave our promise to be model husbands and good cooks.

To Mr. Joseph Kamakau, who patiently guided us to four song contest victories, we leave our sincere aloha and appreciation for his help.

To Mr. Don Mitchell, our class advisor, we leave our deepest aloha for piloting our class safely into port.

We bequeath to the on coming seniors our Senior Cottage (house and lot); our canteen; and the privilege of becoming cadet officers.

To the present low-juniors we leave our ability to "get-along" on our first part-time jobs.

To the "suffer-mores" we leave the honor and privilege of becoming juniors which will make their sufferings less.

To the freshies, we leave our knowledge of social etiquette with the hopes that it will be properly exercised on calling nights.

To the junior division boys we leave our privileges to go off campus.

As individuals we will the following:

I, Joe Anakalea, will my way of "how to get along with women" to Francis Akana, my short legs to Arthur Swift and my nick name "Lepo" to Francis Kauka.

To William Anahu, I, Joe Anuhea, leave in trust with next year's canteen managers, the total sum of one penny (1 cent) to be used only when necessary, primarily, to keep you out of the "Bums" club.

To Edmund Newton, Kenneth Bell leaves his Tarzan tactics with the hope that he will be able to master the chinning bar.

I, Lloyd Ai Chang, leave to William Toomey my doubts about brake lining, and to Arthur "Water Buffalo" Chang my technique of poi slinger.

I, Frank Cockett, bequeath to Clarence "Wimpy" Wilmington my basketball ability, if any, with the assurance that he will develop into a clever instinct shooter; to the mighty and frolic Hui Maninis with their ever present temptations of leaving campus without permission, I bestow upon you, all my luck and happiness in the future; and to Archie Ching I leave my position as houseman in the C. E.

To Rodney Burgess and Lowthian Stern, I, Herbert Dunn, will my part-time room with hopes that they will sweep it at least once every two weeks; my football ability, if any, to Alexander Kahapea; and my electrical technique to Sidney "Pake" Yim, including jobs to be done on the hill.

I, Comfort Eaton, bequeath my basketball ability to Major Desha and my electrical knowledge to Von Hulu Donlin.

To Adrian D'Esmond, I, Folinga Faufata, will my marine and navigating ability, and my art of story telling and joking to William "Bebe" Daniels.

To Manuel Burgess, I, Jacob Haili, will my trumpet with its amber mouthpiece hoping to hear a few intelligible tunes in the near future; to cousin Andrew Boyd, I will my ability to play the sax, with hopes that he may have more sax—appeal.

To Herbert Low, I, Charles Hardee, will my chewing gum; and my free milk nickel sticks to Ralph Miller.

I, Charles Hustace, leave to Charles Ahia my blond hair, and my piano skill to George Pilger.

To the Kamehameha Schools, I, Alonzo Hutchinson, will my tooth pick; my basketball technique and brains to Phoebe Cockett; and my ability of being a mystery to women to Jacob "Jake" Stern.

I, Samuel "Misogynist" Kamakau, bequeath my misogynist membership card and my "women hatred-stuff" to John Hampton Allen, Jr., and my commission as a private to Henry Lum when he graduates.

To Victor Jacobson, I, Joseph Kim, will my ink bottle, and love for baseball with the hopes that they will be properly used and not abused.

I, Ivanhoe McGregor, will my nickname "Mac" to Boyd MacKenzie, my talking and noise to David White so that there won't be any competition against him.

I, Walter Mookini, leave my "dead shot" basket shooting to Alexander Desha.

To Hartwell Blake, I, James Nakapaahu, Jr., leave my unsurpassing leadership; to Maurice Kong I leave my sporting blood; and to Leith Cacares, my unequaled ways with women.

To Henry Ohumukini, I, Soon Kim Tai, bequeath my unsurpassed leadership, if any, as head waiter and my "brodascious" technique of "wolfing."

To Gabriel "Boonic" Victor, I, Edmund "Ticky" Vasconcellos, will my jumping ability with the hopes that he will break all existing Hawaiian records and also, my ability to play tennis.

I, Henry Watson, will my lyric-tenor voice and musical talent to Walter Eli and my art of attracting the weaker sex to Benedict Eleneki.

To Jonathan Kahananui, I, George West, will all my scholastic honors, including the Big Six pin. I also ask him to remember that it "Tisn't" the size that counts.

To Teddy Awana, I, Elmer Williamson, will my woeful wanted knowledge as a buffoonist.

I, James Yim, leave my pliers to the electric shop, my old shoes to "Puka" Frazier, and my combination lock to Dorm "B."

To Lowthian Stern, I, William Yomes, will my crooning powers primarily to keep peace within his dorm; my ability to play the piano to Frank Kernohan; and my drawing ability to Mr. Mansfield Claflin, hoping for the best results.

In witness thereof, we have affixed our signatures to this our last will and testament.

Signed:
CLASS OF 1935

MEMORIES OF HOOLAULEA WEEK END

Left—Supper time at K. S. B. Hoolaulea Day; Right—Governor Joseph B. Poindexter and Principal-in-Charge Homer F. Barnes reviewing Kamehameha battalion.

BOYS' HORRORSCOPE

NAME—	NICKNAME—	DESCRIPTION—	IS—
Joseph Anakalea	Lepo	Short Legs	A Viper
Joseph Anuhea	Big Joe	Cool Headed	Ticklish
Kenneth Bell	Big Body	Chubby	A woman's man
Frank Cockett	Frankie	Big	Absent-minded
Lloyd Chang	Hawk Shaw	Air Flow	Stream-lined
Ernest Dias	Joe Dias Son	Don Juan	Nutty
Herbert Dunn	Small Kid	Small	Crazy at times
Jacob Haili	Jock	Polynesian	Comical
Charles Hardee	Major	Sweet	Business-like
Comfort Eaton	Rufus	Iron Man	A wolf
Folinga Faufata	Samoan	Round	A vagabond
Charles Hustace	Chee Chee	Ehu	Musical
Alonzo Hutchinson	Alfonzo	Solemn	Annoying
Sam Kamakau	Sammie	Bum Knee	Romantic
Joseph Kim	Kemo	Quiet	Studious
Ivanhoe McGregor	Mc	Noisy	Inquisitive
Walter Mookini	Moo	Handsome	Quiet
James Nakapaahu	Nakapee	Two by four	A lefty
Soon Kim Tai	Soo Nee	Dimples	Funny
Edmund Vasconcellos	Tickie	Legs	A bachelor
Henry Watson	Watkens	Muscle bound	A crooner
George West	George	Short	Ambitious
Elmer Williamson	Long Drink	Long legged	Amusing
James Yim	Yabo	Dainty	A Romeo
William Yomes	Bill	Slow	Good Natured

GIRLS' HORRORSCOPE

NAME—	AMBITION—	NICKNAME—	LOVES—
Mele Ainoa	To travel	Spottie	To makes eyes
Marjorie Alo	To retain her girlish figure	Opu	Chop sui
Irene Akeo	To work with children	Flash	Parties
Kaliko Burgess	To be a mannequin to fat women	Squatty	To argue
Beatrice Cockett	To put Paia on the map	Trixie	To osculate
Maile Cockett	To manage the Cockett trio	Pinochio	Wise cracks
Haunani Cooper	To swim the English Channel	Scotty	Swimming
Mary Duvauchelle	To be an operatic star	Duvie	To sing
Mamie Jensen	To own a flower shop	German	Arranging flowers
Eleanor Kaina	To become a singer	Bumpie	To dance
Katherine Kalahui	To work in an office	Uncle Dickie	To cook
Mary Kunane	To know about music aesthetics	Aramy	Nuts
Leinaala Lee	To be a road sweeper	Taffy	To tease
Elsie Long	To live on love	Lala	Hitch hiking
Belle Lowry	To become a nun	Tita	Freedom
Rebecca Macy	To be Major of Nanakuli	Zazu	Unnecessary noise
Madeline Mahoe	To be in the money	Bouncer	To go places
Sarah Maialoha	To be a Red Cross nurse	Bozo	Shows
Gladys Naone	To be a spinster	Kid Chassy	Sports
Ellen Stewart	To be a lawyer	Sis	To be different
Lena Supe	To own the prize elephant	Biggie	Her elephant
Virginia Wo	To own a home in Nuuanu	Bisaiya	A cozy nest
Evelyn Yates	To own a beauty salon	Terlie	Good times

BOYS' HORRORSCOPE

OUGHT TO BE—	AMBITION—	EXPRESSION—
Loved	To be an electrician	Head-ache!
A night watchman	To eat and sleep	Going my way
In a circus	Body builder	"A"—"A"
A black smith	Contractor	N-a-a-a-h!
Vamped	Governor	La-Paree
In the talkies	A big shot	What this?
Hog-tied	A cowpuncher	Hey!
A wrestler	A machinist	How can lose
A radical	Pump engineer	Make me laugh
Married	Flatfoot	Wise guy, eh?
A monk	Sail the seven seas	What this kind
Put out	To dance	Is that so
Killed -to death	To operate a hoe	You can't take it
A preacher	To raise coffee	Go pound sand
Noisier	Own a poi factory	What meaning
Shot	To attend the "U"	Deadheads!
Heard oftener	To raise pigs	How's it Keed!
A farmer	Kauai senator	Alright! Alright!
Stretched a bit	To go to China	Aw!
A Romeo	To jump seven feet	You know me
A politician	To be an orator	I no care
Taller	To be a journalist	How's it
Stepped on	Picture snatcher	Eh, like this
A prohibitionist	Own a beer parlor	You think at's funny
Looked after	Play the piano	Eh, no play

GIRLS' HORRORSCOPE

IS—	OUGHT TO BE—	DESCRIPTION	EXPRESSION—
All smiles	Looked after	Skyscraper	Go home
Noisy	Mama's girl	Happy go lucky	You tell 'em
Always having calls	Tamed	Hardboiled	Can't take it
Fun loving	Taken in hand	Formy	Skip it
Lovesick	A Missionary	Sophisticated	I get a kick
Carefree	A lexicographer	Naughty	Don't be silly
Indifferent	More sociable	Masculine	What about it?
Understanding	A social worker	Plump	Oh Chee, tanks
Dainty	Careless	Dainty	You bet
Talkative	Shushed	Firm	Good Stuff
Insistent	A Phy. Ed. Director	Athletic	I told you so
Serious	Less serious	Visionary	I'll see about it
Studious	In love	Slender	Oh you monkey!
Casual	Sour	Short	Auwe!
Wreckless	Chaperoned	Devilish	Och! Och!
Crazy at times	A Stenographer	Buggie	Us two go dance
Jolly	Chained	Curvy	Oh deah
Militaristic	In the army	A dreamy romancer	Learn you how
A faithful worker	Moonstruck	Solemn	Bugs
Unconcerned	A dictator	Moody	Please be quiet
A livewire	A deadhead	Elongated	Goodness
Ambitious	Big shot	Dignified	Oh cramidy
Hot	Cooled	Just an armful	Saw my honey today

MEMOIRS

MEMOIRS

MEMOIRS

MEMOIRS

MEMOIRS

Ka Buke o Kamehameha

Telling of Life at Kamehameha Schools,

Courses of Study and Opportunities Offered Boys and Girls,

Sports and Activity Program,

Cost of Attending School and General Information.

KAMEHAMEHA FOUNDED IN 1887

Scarcely a half a century ago—less than 50 years—when Hawaii was still a kingdom, Kamehameha Schools were founded.

It was a small beginning—only a few boys being numbered in the group that assembled on the barren campus two miles from Honolulu for the opening day in October, 1887. Not until seven years later was the School for Girls added.

The group may have been small and the campus may have been desolate but the ideals and hopes with which the founders started were high. These ideals were inspired by the royal Bernice Pauahi, princess of the line of Kamehameha, who made possible the founding of the school through bequests in her will.

Her husband, the Honorable Charles R. Bishop, added further substantial contributions.

AIMS OF THE SCHOOL

It was the expressed wish of Princess Pauahi that the "trustees provide first and chiefly a good education in the common English branches, and also instruction in morals and in such useful knowledge as

Kamehameha Schools— Their Past and Present

Each Year Three Hundred and Fifty Boys and Girls Take Advantage of Kamehameha Educational Training

may tend to make good and industrious men and women, and I desire instruction in the higher branches to be subsidiary to the foregoing object."

These wishes have always been the chief goal of the school, every opportunity being given the students to improve their knowledge and to develop their particular abilities.

CHANGES TAKE PLACE

Many changes have taken place during the 50 years that Kamehameha Schools have been in existence. The Kingdom of Hawaii has become a part of the United States and community interests and industries have advanced and changed. So Kamehameha has changed and improved, always remembering its purpose to help boys and girls prepare themselves so that when they finish at Kamehameha and go back to their communities they will be prepared to fit into the life there and be good and industrious citizens.

All over the territory are graduates— alumnae and alumni — of Kamehameha Schools, and these graduates are taking leading positions in their communities. Some of these graduates are teachers, some are legislators, some are judges, some

Hawaiian village at the mouth of Waimea valley, Kauai, in the time of Captain Cook, sketched by Webber.

GEORGE M. COLLINS
Treasurer

JOHN K. CLARKE

RICHARD H. TRENT

ALBERT F. JUDD
Vice-President

Other Members of the Board of Trustees of the Bishop Estate

are business men, some are machinists, some are electricians, some are housewives. So the story goes. Kamehameha graduates are to be found engaged successfully in all sorts of occupations. These graduates are fitting into the life in their communities, and they are doing more. They are helping to improve the territory and make life more enjoyable and more worthwhile—what is called "richer living."

To have a chance to go to Kamehameha is the goal toward which numbers of boys and girls eagerly strive. About four hundred boys and girls took the examinations last spring.

JUNIOR AND SENIOR HIGH SCHOOL

Kamehameha is no longer an elementary school, as it was when it first opened. It now begins with the junior high school year and continues on through the senior high school years. Thus those boys and girls who wish to enter Kamehameha now study carefully in their home town grade schools so they will be able to pass the entrance tests and become members of the growing family of Kamehameha-ites.

MANY TAKE ENTRANCE TESTS

Out of four hundred boys and girls who took entrance examinations last spring only about one hundred could be admitted to Kamehameha. The result of the entrance tests was only one of the factors that determined who should be admitted to Kamehameha.

One of the other things that helped the entrance committee decide whether a pupil was allowed to enroll at Kamehameha was the previous school record of the pupil applying for admission. The character rating of the pupil, his ambition, his industry, his willingness to work, and his background were all considered by the entrance committee. If the committee finally felt that the pupil would profit by coming to Kamehameha and had the possibilities of making a social contribution, as many other Kamehameha graduates have done in various life activities in their communities, it recommended him for admission.

SOME DAY PUPILS ACCEPTED

Kamehameha is a boarding school—although a few day pupils are accepted—and it is the home of the boys and girls for about nine months out of the year.

DR. HOMER F. BARNES
Principal-in-charge
of Kamehameha Schools

Hence there is much to life at Kamehameha besides classroom and studies and recitations. If the boys and girls are going to become the good and industrious citizens that Mrs. Bishop wished, it is necessary that opportunities be offered the students for experience in leadership, fair play, learning to live with others, and learning the proper social manners.

SCHOOL IS HOME TO STUDENTS

Since the school is home to the students, and the dormitory masters and house mothers try to take the place of fathers and mothers, many of these experiences are offered naturally in daily meetings in the dormitory, around the tables in the common dining hall at mealtime, and on the play fields or in the various organizations.

The School for Boys is located on one campus and the School for Girls on another and, while they have many activities in common, their organization and daily programs are somewhat different.

Bishop Hall, where the School for Boys classes are held.

Many other schools have grown up since Kamehameha was started, but Kamehameha is particularly dear to the hearts of Hawaiians. Today enrolled in the school are many sons and daughters or other relatives of former Kamehameha students.

A Sunday dress review put on by the Kamehameha School for Boys battalion.

One of the dormitories at the School for Girls. Teachers and girls live together in a homelike atmosphere.

Photo by Seventh Photo Section, A. C., Luke Field, T. H.

Kamehameha Schools from the air. The Boys' School in the foreground and the Girls' School on Kapalama Heights in the background.

THE FIRST DAY AT THE SCHOOL FOR BOYS

When the boy first comes to the School for Boys in the fall he goes to Bishop Hall —that old stone building where the fathers of many of the boys once also went to school—to register and receive his dormitory room assignment. Later he goes to the business office—which is in the building where the Boys Preparatory School was located for more than 40 years—and pays his tuition and fees for school activities, medical attention, and uniform.

After completing these arrangements, the boy draws his room equipment from the armory. In his dormitory the older boys show him how to arrange his room properly and tell him about the school program. The dormitory master, who lives in one part of the dormitory, is on hand to help in any way he can. There are five dormitories, two cottages and two lanais on the boys' campus, making room for about 200 boarders.

DAILY ACTIVITIES VARIED

The daily activities of the boy at Kamehameha are so different from day to day as to be ever interesting.

The stirring notes of a bugle call will awaken the boy at 6 o'clock in the morning, but many of the youngsters are already up and ready to go before the bugler makes his appeal. The boys wash and assemble on the road that winds in front of

School for Boys Courses Open Many Opportunities
Pupils Receive Well-Balanced Training While Learning to Take Their Places in Their Local Communities

A general science class at the School for Boys in the science laboratory.

In the electric shop at the School for Boys.

Dormitories A and B. The companies then go through brisk setting-up exercises while the younger boys engage in tumbling stunts in the gymnasium.

Breakfast call sends everyone hurrying to the dining hall. After breakfast the boys return to their dormitories and clean their rooms, make their beds, and generally put the dormitory in order for the morning inspection which is made by the dormitory master and the senior officer shortly after 7 o'clock. At 7:25 morning assembly begins, in Bishop Hall. These assembly programs are of many kinds—talks by faculty members, addresses by outside speakers or entertainers, student programs, and group singing. The one requisite for these assemblies is that they be interesting, for without interest there is little learning.

CLASSES HELD IN THE MORNING

Classes begin at 7:45 and last until 12:10, when a recess of an hour is allowed for lunch. At 1:15 classes are resumed, ending at 2. At 2:15 the daily work period begins, when the boys take part in cleaning dormitories, mowing lawns and otherwise keeping their homes in order, just as they would at home anywhere else.

Following the 45-minute work period there is a special class period for those students who are behind in their studies. After this period there is a

two-hour period given over to the various games played between dormitories. A football league is arranged for the dorm boys in the fall, and late in the year other games are played. Since some of the younger boys are not strong enough to play in the dorm league, a special football league is arranged for them. Later, basketball, volleyball, tennis, track, swimming, and other sports are held for all. Every boy at Kamehameha has a chance to play in the games he likes and to learn about new ones. He also competes with boys of approximately his own physical development.

R. O. T. C. TRAINING

The School for Boys has regular Reserve Officer Training Corps military training. The boys learn how to march, how to command, and how to handle a rifle. The Kamehameha battalion, which may be seen smartly stepping along to the stirring strains of the popular Kamehameha band in Armistice Day, Memorial Day, and other special occasion parades, is one of which all friends of Kamehameha are proud.

The Senior boys are the officers, the two boys who have displayed the greatest promise of intelligent leadership winning the much-desired honor of being Cadet Majors. The commanding officers of each company select from the School for Girls one girl for each company as honorary sponsor. These girls, in attractive blue and white uniforms, march with the bat-

A group of boys during the daily work period. Each boy takes part in cleaning the dormitory and helping keep the campus neat and clean.

talion on special occasions. The Sunday dress reviews which the battalion puts on during the spring are attended by hundreds of Honolulu people.

SCHOOL HELPS IN VOCATIONAL CHOICE

Sooner or later every boy realizes that he has to decide what he is going to do to make a living after he leaves school. Many boys make this decision without much preparation and get into some sort of work which they cannot do very well and which they do not like.

The Kamehameha School for Boys knows that this is likely to happen, so it plans to help the boy make the right choice. In order to have this plan work out, each boy is given a chance to work in each of the different vocational shops while he is in the lower grades so that he can pick out the work he likes best.

BOYS EXPLORE VOCATIONS

The vocations which a boy is allowed to explore are electricity, carpentry, auto mechanics, machinist, forging and welding, and agriculture. By the time he reaches the Tenth Grade he has a fairly clear idea as to the vocation he likes best. Then he talks over his plans with his instructors and finally, after careful consideration of his special interests and aptitudes, makes his vocational choice. From then on he devotes several periods a week to doing special shop work in the line he has chosen, gradually taking up more training.

Seventh Grade (rear row)—A. Johnson, J. Banning, H. Puu, B. Awana, Mr. Jones, L. Holt, R. Moss, G. Pilger, W. Paikuli.

(Front row)—J. Sims, A. Miyamoto, A. Chang, R. Muller, C. Christ, S. Desha, L. Brown, I. Hanchett.

Eighth Grade (rear row)—V. Colburn, F. Aiona, J. Kaina, J. Blevins, V. Boyd, W. Wilson, D. Alama, J. Mattson, J. Kekahu, H. Brandt.

(Middle row)—C. Benham, E. Holt, J. Morrison, R. Hart, J. Simonson, A. Desha, G. Baker, H. Low, Wray Taylor, A. Ernst.

(Front row)—R. Dreier, K. Silveira, J. Puu, G. Stender, J. Gomard, H. Choy, A. Kekai, S. Guerrero, J. Aki, A. Parker.

BOYS EXPERIENCE REAL SITUATION

If he is in the electric shop, he has the opportunity to make various electrical repairs and improvements needed on the campus, such as installing bell systems, rigging up lights, or looking after electrical machinery.

If he is in the auto mechanics shop, he will repair damaged cars. One way of learning repairs which the boys always like is for the instructor to damage secretly some part of one of the several old cars used for experiments and to send the boys out about the campus with it. Their problem is to repair the car and bring it back to the shop after it breaks down.

At the School for Boys dining hall.

Boys working on shop projects. Above—Auto mechanics department; right—investigating in the engineering shop.

And so with each shop. The boys get to work on practical problems while learning to become skilled in the trades they have selected.

PART-TIME TRAINING PLAN USED

In order to make more certain that a boy will be able to get work when he finishes school, Kamehameha has adopted the part-time training plan known as the Antioch plan. This means that for two years the boy will spend part of his time in school and part of his time on some real job. Various business firms on the Island of Oahu work with the school on this project. For two weeks the boy goes to

Ninth Grade (rear row)—F. Strohlin, E. Hulihee, H. Kunewa, H. Vida, S. Martinson, C. Iona, I. Kaopua, T. Wilcox.
(3rd row)—H. Morse, J. Kalani, W. L. Seto, M. Burgess, H. Hussey, J. Awana, J. Palk, W. Chang, Mr. Wise.
(2nd row)—G. Lee, F. Vaughan, E. Doyle, C. Plunkett, S. Hazelwood, C. Mokiao, E. Amona, S. Yim, R. Mahikoa, L. Weight.
(Front row)—H. Miyamoto, E. Huddy, C. Rosecrans, J. Kahananui, J. Chun, H. Ho, W. Daniels, E. Kekai.
Tenth Grade (rear row)—H. Naone, John Akana, M. Pei, R. Jellings, R. Colburn, B. MacKenzie, R. Hubbell, C. Braun.
(3rd row)—R. Friel, W. Eli, D. Kalama, J. Naone, J. Yoshida, A. Swift, J. Wood, Mr. W. B. Caldwell.
(2nd row)—S. Williams, C. Branco, J. Naehu, I. Ahue, G. Akana, S. Kahalewai, A. Todd, J. Fitzgerald.
(Front row)—J. Akim, G. Kekauoha, D. White, R. Lutz, H. Harris, J. Akima, J. Allen.

Top—Cadet officers of Section B, Kamehameha School Battalion. (Left to right)—Joseph Anuhea, Comfort Eaton (major), James Nakapaahu, Soon Kim Tai, Herbert Dunn, Folinga Faufata, Charles Hustace, Ernest Dias, Lloyd Ai Chang, Alonzo Hutchinson.

Center—Cadet officers, Section A (left to right)—Charles Hardee (major), Kenneth Bell, James Yim, Jacob Haili, Joseph Kim, Walter Mookini, Frank Cockett.

Kamehameha Schools Cadet Band.

Right—High Chief Abner Paki, father of Princess Bernice Pauahi Bishop.

Left—High Chiefess Konia, mother of Princess Bernice Pauahi Bishop.

Photographs Courtesy Bishop Museum

school, attending his regular classes. Then the next two weeks he works as a regular employee with some firm.

BALANCED COURSE PRESENTED

Boys receive regular wages while on their part-time jobs, so they are able to pay a good part of their school expenses during their final two years at Kamehameha. Doing the actual jobs in his chosen vocation gives the boy just the right sort of preparation so he will be able to hold a regular job when he finishes school. Many of the boys fit so well into their part-time work that they are kept on as regular employees by the firms after being graduated from Kamehameha.

A boy needs to know many things today besides how to perform some vocational task. Knowing how to talk correctly and how to read and write well are very important, if he is to fit into life after he leaves school.

The teachers are with the boys in many places on the campus besides in the classroom and are always trying to help the pupils improve their use of English. On the play field the teachers act as coaches, in the dormitories as housemasters, in the din-

ing room as hosts, in the club meetings as advisers—always on hand to assist in the use of correct English as well as ready to help the boys with the many boy problems and difficulties that arise.

ENGLISH TRAINING IMPORTANT

One of the things the boys receive help in as part of their English classes is the discovery of new and interesting books to read. Many poems, short stories and novels are intensely interesting, but many boys never find them. The English teachers know about these books and help each boy to explore and find the type of read-

Low-Eleven Agriculture Shop boys, with the gift of chickens recently received from the mainland.

KAMEHAMEHA
SCHOOLS

ing that he likes best.

Knowledge of figures, so as to do the many daily mathematical problems he will encounter in handling his own affairs after he leaves school, is another valuable asset. The student bank where the pupils keep their spending money, to be checked out each week as needed, is very helpful in teaching boys the value of saving and the use of checks. .

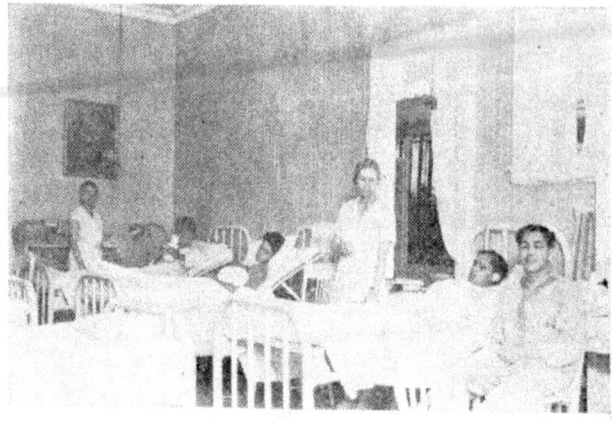

The School for Boys infirmary, where trained nurses watch over the health of the boys.

SCIENCE COURSES INCLUDED

If a boy is going to understand his vocation well enough to get ahead in it, he must know about mechanical drawing so he can work out plans; and, likewise, he needs to know about physics, which teaches about the natural laws that control the forces with which he works in his vocation.

General science and biology help one to live properly. Men of science are finding out more about life every day. They are discovering more about disease and how to prevent and cure various diseases and in the science classes the pupils in turn find out about these things.

Diet and proper care of one's body are stressed.

Seniors in the special homemaking class for boys at the School for Girls. Cooking, budgeting and various other valuable information on how to conduct one's home are taught.

LEARNING HOW TO LIVE WITH PEOPLE

Social science shows how the people of the past lived and helps those of the present learn how to enjoy living with one another. A keen interest in national and international affairs is developed in social science classes by keeping up with world events through daily newspapers. When election time comes, voting is studied and practiced just as it is to be done when each boy becomes 21 years of age and votes in real elections. What to consider in deciding for whom to vote is worked out in the classes. Of especial interest to Hawaiian boys and girls is the class in Hawaiian history and culture for senior students. This is different from any other class in the school and much different from the usual type of class found in any school. Instead of having a regular class period, the boys and girls meet one evening a week and listen to some outside man or woman tell about some side of ancient Hawaiian life which he or she knows best. When studying the plant life of ancient Hawaii the pupils meet out of doors in the Hawaiian grove on the road to the School

High-Eleventh grade—rear row (left to right)—Francis Kauka, Irving Maby, William Toomey, Benedict Eleneki, Theodore Awana, Archie Ching, Herbert Cockett, James Carroll, Eugene Burke.

(Front row)—Adrian D'Esmond, Leilehua Naumu, Hartwell Blake, Maurice Kong, Henry Lum, Charles Ahia, Henry Mahikoa, Gabriel Victor, Alexander Kahapea, Paul Frendo, Henry Ohumukini.

Low-Eleventh grade—rear row (left to right)—Edward Namilimili, Arthur Betts, Llewellyn Strohlin, Louis Suares, Stewart Markham, George Kahanu, Major Desha, Victor Jacobson, Frederick Lee, Aki Kini Levi Pea, Allan Akana.

(Middle row)—Mr. C. V. Budd, Samuel K. Kalama, Albert Akana, Charles Kaninau, Cecil Kiilehua, Alexander In, Charles Mahoe, Kaena Nahale-a, Manuel Sproat, Arthur Harris, Matthew Lee Loy.

(Front row)—Charles Bailey, James Akana, Edmund Newton, Von Hulu Donlin, Richard Kong, Clarence Wilmington, Jacob Stern, Leith Caceres, William Like.

for Girls and wander through the grove, learning about the plants as in olden days when the makua went into the forest with the pupil.

FIELD TRIPS PART OF COURSES

All these things mentioned are brought out in the courses at the School for Boys. Visits by classes to various places off the campus help the pupils see how the things they learn in their courses apply to life outside of school.

SONG CONTEST ALWAYS POPULAR

The School for Boys' annual Song Contest is a high point in the music year. All interest centers in the perfecting of the singing in the special songs each class sings, many parents and alumni offering their services to help boys reach that perfection for which Kamehameha singing is famous.

This past year the idea of having special costumes and stage settings to add to the effect of the songs by each group proved very popular with the classes. Held as the contests are, out of doors at night, the harmonious singing of the various

groups never fails to thrill the hundreds who attend.

Kamehameha singing groups are always in demand for outside appearances and for radio numbers. The boys top off their year of music with their appearance in the annual combined Glee Clubs concert with the girls. So popular is this affair that seats are always difficult to obtain.

HEALTH OF BOYS WATCHED WITH CARE

Kamehameha wants a boy to be healthy and happy in school and after he leaves school. In order to make this possible the school helps the boys learn how to prevent illness as well as cure it. Various tests and examinations are given frequently to make sure the pupils are well. If a pupil is ill or is not strong, his work and activities are arranged so as to build the body. Special diets and activity programs are arranged for underweight boys. The school has a school infirmary where boys who are ill receive treatment and attention from skilled nurses. For severe illness or accident the pupil is sent to the city hospital. A school doctor and a dentist visit the school regularly to examine the

A church of yesterday—drawing of old Hawaiian heiau.

pupils and come when needed for emergency cases.

STUDY HELP PLAN USED

When a pupil is having difficulty in some particular subject, he is given an extra study period with his instructor. Close personal attention given this way helps pupils gain a better foundation in all subjects.

A happy interested boy gains much from his school life. The whole K. S. B. program is arranged with this in mind and Kamehameha helps the boy in his attitudes as well as in his studies. If the boy has an individual difficulty he is given especial consideration and the Faculty members try to help him find a solution to his problem. Every boy has problems that are just a little bit different from those of other boys so every boy receives carefully considered attention for his own particular difficulties.

DISCIPLINE TEACHES LAW AND ORDER

Discipline of some sort is necessary to keep law and order anywhere and Kamehameha has discipline to help the boys realize the need to coöperate in school

Winners of the Halloween prizes at the 1934 senior division party.

life, just as they need to coöperate in life outside of school. As in building the proper attitudes toward school work, so in the discipline attention is given to each individual boy. Discipline is administered not to punish the boy but to help him realize the offense and help him improve so he will not make the same mistake again. Every effort is made to help each boy, but in some rare cases boys refuse to coöperate. If, after every effort has been tried, the school feels that the boy is not benefiting by remaining at Kamehameha, he is urged to try a new environment.

A church of today—Bishop Memorial Chapel, a gift from the Hon. C. R. Bishop.

COURSES OF STUDY—SCHOOL FOR BOYS

Seventh Grade

Subject	Periods per week	Instructor
English	7	Mr. Sather
Social Science	6	Mr. D. Bailey
Mathematics	6	Mr. Caldwell
Shop	6	Mr. Burmeister and Mr. Jones
Music	3	Mr. Kernohan
Mechanical Drawing	3	Mr. Jones
Shop Understanding	1	Mr. Jones
Library	5	

Eighth Grade

English	6	Mr. Sather
Social Science	6	Mr. Stone
Mathematics	5	Mr. Caldwell
Elementary Science	3	Mr. Mitchell
Shop	6	Mr. Budd and Mr. Claflin
Music	3	Mr. Sather
Shop Understanding	1	Mr. Burmeister
Orientation	1	Dr. Barnes
Mechanical Drawing	3	Mr. Lowrie
Library	3	

Ninth Grade

English	5	Mr. Ebey
Mathematics	5	Mr. Caldwell
General Science	5	Mr. Mitchell
Civics	3	Mr. Church
Music	2	Mr. Kernohan
Orientation	1	Dr. Barnes
Shop	11	Various Instructors
Mechanical Drawing	3	Mr. Lowrie
Library	2	

Tenth Grade

English	5	Mr. Ebey
Biology	5	Mr. Mitchell
Social Science	5	Mr. Stone, Mr. Hudson
Typing	3	Mr. A. Bailey
Military Science	1	Lt. Hinds
Orientation	1	Dr. Barnes
Shop	11	Various instructors
Music	2	Mr. Kernohan
Mechanical Drawing	2	Mr. Lowrie
Library	2	

Low-Eleventh Grade

English	5	Mr. Hudson
Physics	5	Mr. Lowrie
Social Science	5	Mr. Church
Typing	3	Mr. A. Bailey
Military Science	1	Lt. Hinds
Orientation	1	Dr. Barnes
Shop	11	Various instructors
Music	2	Mr. Kernohan
Mechanical Drawing	2	Mr. Lowrie
Library	2	

High-Eleventh Grade

English	6	Mr. Shepardson
Business Arithmetic	5	Mr. A. Bailey
Plane Geometry	5	Mr. D. Bailey
Military Science	1	Lt. Hinds
Orientation	1	Dr. Barnes
Shop	11	Various instructors
Music	2	Mr. Kernohan
Mechanical Drawing	3	Mr. Lowrie
Library	3	

Twelfth Grade

English	6	Mr. Shepardson
Social Science	5	Mr. Church
Business Arithmetic or Plane Geometry	5	Mr. A. Bailey or Mr. D. Bailey
Military Science	1	Lt. Hinds
Orientation	1	Dr. Barnes
Shop	11	Various instructors
Music	2	Miss Brown and Mr. Kernohan
Homemaking or Mechanical Drawing	3	Miss Auman, Miss Hirleman or Mr. Lowrie
Library	3	

A lineup of the crack junior basketball team coached by Mr. Clarence V. Budd of K. S. B. which won the junior interscholastic championship.

SCHOOL FOR BOYS FACULTY

Allan A. Bailey   Donald W. Bailey   Claude G. Banning   Clarence V. Budd   Edward R. Burmeister

William B. Caldwell   Miss Maude Chambers   Alfred M. Church   Mansfield P. Claflin   George W. Ebey

Sgt. Dale Frazier   Lt. Sidney R. Hinds   Loring G. Hudson   Mrs. Laura Johnson   William P. Jones

Frank P. Kernohan   Robert H. Lowrie   Donald D. Mitchell   Charles T. Parrent   N. Kenneth Sather

Rowland R. Shepardson   Daniel Stone   Miss Bertha Van Auken   Miss Ruth Winstedt   William S. Wise

SCHOOL FOR GIRLS FACULTY

Miss Maude E. Schaeffer
Principal

Miss Margaret Auman

Mrs. Marcella Ballengee

Milton E. Ballengee

Miss Daisy Bell

Miss Caroline Bissinger

Miss Gertrude Bolton

Miss Laura E. Brown

Miss Mabel Catlin

Miss Pauline Frederick

Miss Emma Garrison

Miss Neva Hirleman

Miss Marguerite Judson

Miss Genevieve Lill

Miss Esther Mahelona

Miss Katherine Moeller

Miss Norma Olsen

Miss Mary Stimson

Miss Mary Wallace

Mrs. Florence Weatherbee

Miss Winifred Wing

Miss Nelle Word

The secret desire of every girl who has had the pleasure of visiting the campus of the School for Girls on Kapalama Heights is to become one of the boarders there. Many girls who have not seen the beautiful stone buildings and pleasant surroundings of flowers and shrubs—all looking out on an always-thrilling view from Diamond Head to the Waianae Range and far to sea— also hope to become members of the Kamehameha family.

School for Girls Trains Pupils in Many Fields

Vocational Opportunities as Well as Homemaking Experiences Offered in Courses at the New School for Girls

The School for Girls, which was first opened in 1894 on the King Street campus, has been in its new home for four years. The new campus is a part of the same Kapalama Ahupuaa that runs, after the traditions of old Hawaii, from the sea to the peaks of the mountains. The King Street campus where the School for Boys is still located is on the lowland part of this ahupuaa.

Back of the School for Girls, stretching up to the summit of the Koolau Range, is additional Bishop Estate land. Although this is a water reserve, its many trails are

A School for Girls sports group with Haleakala Hale, the dining hall which also houses the K. S. G. offices and a number of classrooms, in the background.

open to the adventurous boys and girls who enjoy hiking. Here each year the younger classes hold special Arbor Day festivities and plant groves of trees.

After each girl has finished the first day's business of registration when school opens, she has a chance to explore the dormitory in which she is to live. There she is shown the room that is to be her very own for the coming year. Soon she meets the girls and teachers who are to be her sisters and mothers in this pleasant new home.

Each morning the girls have their devotion services, for which the Faculty and various classes take turns preparing programs. Sometimes there are outside speakers or musicians.

Classes last until 12:40, then there is recess for lunch. At mealtimes all the girls gather in Haleakala Hale and together with the faculty members eat their meals at tables where older girls act as hostesses. Haleakala Hale was so named in memory of the home

Seniors in the School for Girls home management cottage. The girls experience real home activities, including preparing and serving of meals during the

nine-week period each girl spends at the cottage. Here, too, the girls receive training in budgeting their money as well as their leisure time.

Girls at K. S. G. receive practical experience in caring for the sick, under supervision of trained nurses.

land Girl Scout conference are also sent during the summer vacation by the K. S. G. troop.

The Campfire Girls club gives the younger girls a chance to give service and find happiness through the activities centered around the Seven Crafts—Home, Health, Handcraft, Nature Lore, Camping, Business, and Citizenship.

MANY HOBBIES ENCOURAGED

Much fun is found by the girls who are members of the Stamp Club and the Kodak Club. The first organization engages in that fascinating hobby of saving stamps and learning about them. The Kodak girls take pictures and then develop the negatives and print pictures in the school dark room which has all facilities for printing and enlarging as well as developing.

In addition to these clubs are extended

of Mr. and Mrs. Bishop, which was renowned for its hospitality and for being a popular meeting place for young people.

GIRLS' CLUBS MEET WEDNESDAYS

Afternoons have varied activities. On Wednesdays after lunch the clubs meet for their projects. Some of the older girls belong to the Girl Reserve organization, the aim of which is to help the girls develop character and social graces. Each summer this group, through funds raised during the school year, sends delegates to the big conference at Asilomar on the mainland.

The Girl Scout troop at the School for Girls is proud of the fact that it is the first troop to have been organized in the Hawaiian Islands. Delegates to the main-

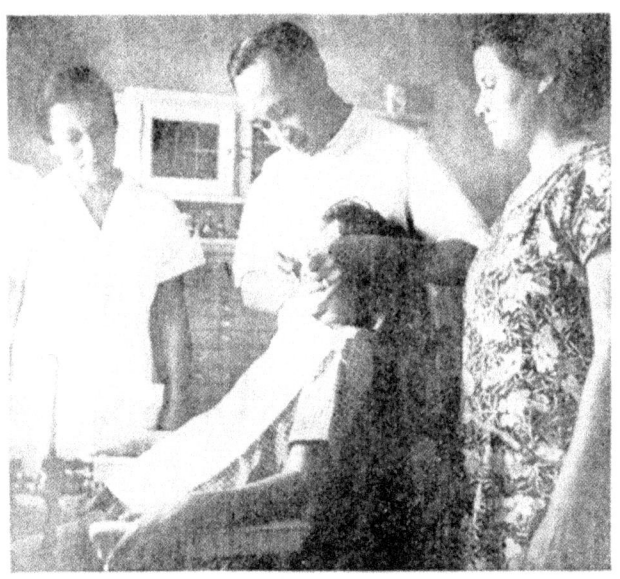

The K. S. G. dentist gives careful attention to the teeth and keeps them in perfect condition.

Seventh Grade (rear row)—Mrs. M. Ballengee, Flora Salm, Pauline Duvauchelle, Frances Weir, Pauline Mookini, Lydia Afat, Rachel Gonsalves, Abigail Bode.

(Front row)—Louise Akana, Macedes Boyd, Sarah Ann Hart, Frances Nohoikaiu, Charlotte Supe, Alice Chang, Eleanor Fountain, Bernice Campbell, Elizabeth Ernst, Hester Adams.

Eighth Grade (rear row)—Angeline Spencer, Dorothy Atcherley, Mary Louise Cobb-Adams, Jacqueline Liwai, Miss M. Wallace, Ulwin Garcia, Leah Chillingworth, May Bode, Sheba Cathcart, Piilani Maxfield, Nohea Kalaluhi.

(Middle row)—Loretta Aiona, Emelia Akeo, Eloise Akana, Winifred Cheong, Helen Boozer, Nancy Punohu, Mabel Heu, Ruby Pua, Ruth Burgess.

(Front row)—Elizabeth Stewart, Dorothy Goo, Mabel Bode, Joan Chalmers, Carolyn Baker.

departmental activities, e. g., the Glee Club, Applied Arts, Sewing Club, and Garden Club, in some of which the girls add to their spending money by selling articles they make.

K. S. G. PUPILS LEARN TO CARE FOR HOMES

Learning to care for a home properly and do all those things that help to make for happiness in the home is one of the big things that the Kamehameha girls do.

Naturally, a part of this learning is finding out how to use the English language properly, obtaining a knowledge of subjects such as social science, general science, biology, gaining skill in such home activities as sewing, cooking, and the like. Many of these ideas and skills are gained not just by sitting in a chair in a classroom for 45 minutes at a time, but by taking part in the actual home life of the school.

MODEL KITCHEN FOR LEARNING COOKING

Thus the girls spend periods in the kitchen where they learn to prepare food

Piano pupils at the School for Girls in front of the main entrance stairway near W. O. Smith Hall.

properly; they wait on tables; they prepare budgets; they make dresses for themselves from patterns of their own selection. They do their own washing and ironing and care for their own rooms. Many earn "pin-money" by doing laundry work for other girls and faculty members.

Girls Reserves, who learn service by actually practicing service.

Left—A corner of the K. S. G. campus; right—The main entrance doors to Haleakala Hale at K. S. G.

Through their home hygiene classes they learn how to care for the sick and how best to prevent illness. Normal problems that are likely to arise in their own homes are discussed and the girls learn what to do in such situations. Every junior girl works one day a week for a semester in the city health clinics.

One of the things which the girls eagerly look forward to when their senior year comes, is the weeks they spend in the Senior Practice Cottage, which is just what the name sounds like. It is a practice home. The girls move into the cottage and practice living in a home. With them lives a teacher who is their "mother" for this time.

REAL HOME LIFE IN PRACTICE COTTAGE

A few weeks' old infant is brought to live in the cottage and the girls learn how to care for a baby. Usually the baby is the child of a graduate of the school. But

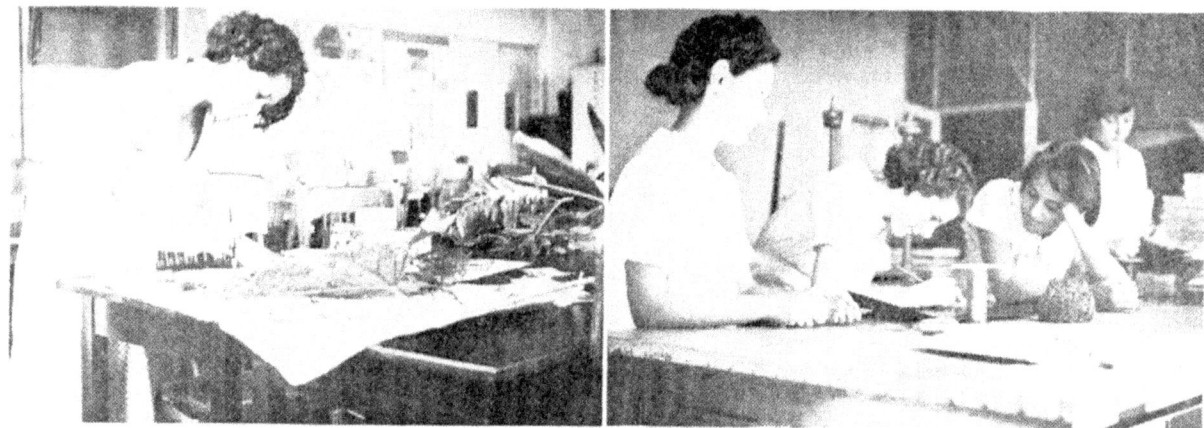

School for Girls students from the art classes. Left—drawing a design; right—tooling leather in bookbinding and leathercraft shop.

School for Girls Honorary Sponsors for Cadet Battalion.
Left to right—Mikahala White, Phoebe Cockett, Lena Supe, Kaliko Burgess, Mamie Jensen.

ried course in this work. Senior girls gain practical experience through part-time jobs with local business firms.

Practice teaching is available to the Seniors through taking charge of Sunday School classes in various churches in the city, and through positions with Castle Kindergarten.

A further vocation the girls may learn is printing, training being given a limited group of Junior and Senior girls in the school print shop. This is a recent idea, but a very successful one, as all the girls trained have

this is not all. The girls also cook their own meals. They invite outside guests and prepare the meals, entertain, and otherwise learn to act as they would in their own homes. Budgets are arranged and the expense kept within the required limits. Each girl takes her turn at the various duties of the household so she may gain experience in all the things she will need to know after she leaves school and makes her own home.

VOCATIONAL OPPORTUNITIES OPEN

Since all girls may not intend to be homemakers, other vocational work is offered to meet other plans. Some girls prefer commercial training, so there is a va-

Some of the students learning printing at the Kamehameha Schools Print Shop.

Tenth Grade (Upper row—left to right)—Katherine Haake, Wilhelmina Baker, Peggy Burkett, Beatrice Vasconcellos, Catherine Sims, Eleanor Horsewill, Ruth Crowell, Mr. Ballengee, Allane Paris, Juanita Wong, Lucille Barringer, Janet Kelii, Mildred Medeiros, Isabella Aiona, Ruth Diffen.

(Lower row)—Margaret Miller, Winona Kanahele, Margaret Kalahui, Emma Macy, Hermine Dreier, Gertrude Kamakau, Nina Abdul, Minerva Carroll, Leilani Lee, Leilehua Toomey, Euphemia Spencer, Mary Yates, Elizabeth Haia, Louise De Arce.

Ninth Grade (Upper row—left to right)—Lilinoe Wilson, Sarah Henrickson, Margaret Dunn, Margaret Clarke, Evelyn Rabideau, Eloise Lanham, Juanita Supe, Wynona Kaiama, Nora Stewart, Bernice Mundon, Anita Thompson, Florence Spahn.

(Lower row)—Miss Margaret Auman, Idamae Sims, Lulu Pali, Mae Spencer, Frances Afat, Helene Cathcart, Louise Kauahilo, Rose-Pearle Kinslea, Elizabeth Akana, Dora Beyer, Evelyn Dias, Thelma Haia, Hannah Goo.

Eleventh Grade (Upper row—left to right)—Eunice Cockett, Anna Duvauchelle, Sybil Mahikoa, Muriel Swift, Georgiana Bishaw, Leilani Allen, Harriet Awana, Ethlyene Sanborn, Katherine Spencer, Cornelia Kamakau, Marjorie Kunewa, Miss P. Frederick, Lily Wilson, Eva Parker, Hazel Goo, Wilma Barringer, Gertrude Williamson.

(Front row)—Audrey Robinson, Stella Kaaua, Luella Mahikoa, Eula Benham, Mikahala White, Phoebe Cockett, Thelma Kauka, Dorothy Kahananui, Katherine Sakuma, Maidie Kaiama, Hilda Mattson, Ululani Weight, Rachel Mahikoa.

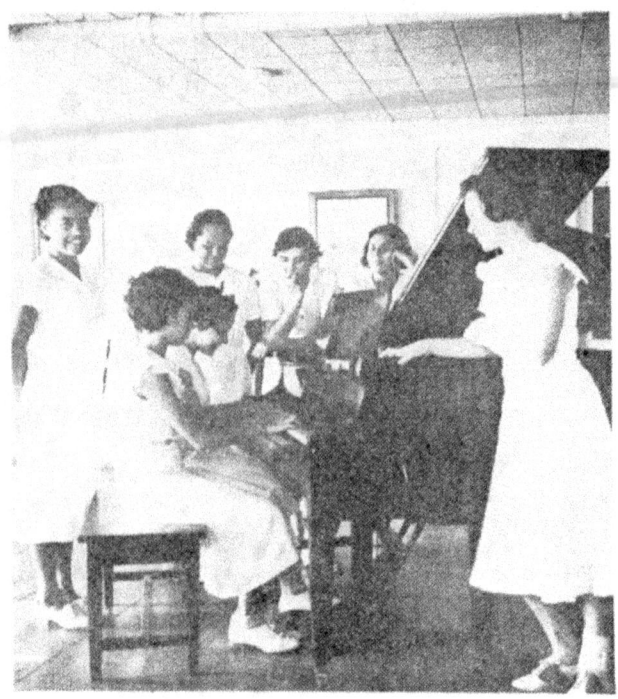

Music is an important part of life at Kamehameha.

been placed in positions and a demand has been made for more.

Another field of endeavor for K. S. G. students is weaving. The first weaving classes in the islands were offered at Kamehameha Girls' School.

A girl needs to know something about art in order to arrange her home pleasantly, so there are art classes and an Art Club for those girls who have more than the ordinary interest in this activity field.

One of the things the art students have done is to make linoleum block designs for Christmas cards and sell these cards.

Through the school bank, where the girls keep their spending money, they learn the value of money, how to handle checks and meet many of the problems connected with money matters which they will encounter when they leave school.

Honolulu has many spots of interest which have a connection with school activities, and the girls frequently visit such institutions as the Academy of Arts and Bishop Museum while studying their various courses. These field trips, as they are called, make understanding of the school work much easier.

LIBRARY A POPULAR, PLEASANT SPOT

W. O. Smith Hall is a popular spot on the School for Girls campus. Here the li-

Combined play periods at the School for Girls are arranged for Friday afternoons for boys and girls.

brary is located, with its many books on all sorts of subjects, its different magazines, and its pleasant reading opportunities. In this same building is the Bookbinding Shop. Many a girl has found pleasant and valuable diversion engaging in some of the many things to do there, such as making leather key cases, memory books, bill folds, and other articles. Many a much-appreciated Christmas gift has come from this shop. Then, too, the Bookbinding and Leathercraft trade offers opportunities for girls after they finish at Kamehameha.

VARIOUS GAMES ARRANGED

All girls like to play games and all girls get a chance to at Kamehameha. The different classes are divided into groups to play hockey, indoor baseball, volley ball, basketball, and soccer. Certain afternoons are arranged for girls who wish to go swimming or to go to the School for Boys campus to play tennis. A chance for all the boys and girls to get acquainted is arranged by having combined play periods on Friday afternoons.

DANCING CLUB TRAINS IN GRACEFULNESS

Learning how to move gracefully is taught effectively through dancing, so a Dancing Club is arranged for those girls especially interested. Sometimes special dance dramas are presented with large numbers of the girls taking part.

SINGING OF KAMEHAMEHA PUPILS WELL LIKED

The singing of Kamehameha students

One of the girls with the practice cottage baby. Learning to care for an infant properly is part of the home-management training each Senior girl experiences.

is especially famous all through the Hawaiian Islands. It is also particularly popular right among the students themselves at school. Each year in the fall the Song Contest is conducted. Each class prepares a special song of its own choice, a general song that all classes in the division are to sing, and an original song.

The night of the contest is one of fever-heat excitement. Parents and other friends of Kamehameha crowd into the gymnasium—Kaahumanu Hale, so named for one of the great alii of Kamehameha history. Storms of applause greet the efforts of each class and the final decision of the judges is met with shrieks of approval,

Keopuolani Hale—the Senior Practice Cottage at the School for Girls.

the winning classes of the Junior and Senior divisions being overwhelmed with congratulations.

PIANO AND VOCAL LESSONS GIVEN

The music activities include both singing and piano music. The piano students give frequent musical teas in which the vocal students also take part. In the spring the grand climax of music for the year is the combined Glee Clubs concert in which both boys and girls take part.

A project of keen interest in the spring is the annual health week program sponsored by the Sophomore Class.

Home to the girls means the three dormitories—Kapiolani Nui Hale, Kekauluohi Hale, and Kinau Hale. The names for most of the buildings on the new campus have been taken from names of great women of the Kamehameha dynasty.

Not every girl knows exactly what she wants to do when she first enters Ka-

Scenes from two outdoor dramatic productions presented by the boys and girls.

mehameha, so a number of courses are arranged to let each girl explore certain activities and find out which she likes best. Then, beginning with the Tenth Grade, the school work is divided into three divisions——the General Course for those who wish to prepare themselves for management of a home; the Commercial Course for those who wish to receive training in stenographic or secretarial work; the Vocational Course, in which the girl may elect to take Bookbinding and Leathercraft training, Weaving or Typing, in addition to certain academic subjects.

—Photo Courtesy Bishop Museum

A sketch made by a visiting French artist showing Kinau, then premier, accompanied by attendants. One of the K. S. G. dormitories has been named Kinau Hale, honoring this alii of the Kamehameha line.

COURSES OF STUDY—SCHOOL FOR GIRLS

Subject	Periods per week	Instructor	Subject	Periods per week	Instructor
Grade VII			Art	2	Miss Wing
English	5	Mrs. Ballengee	Cooking (one semester)	6 (or 3 for year)	Miss Bell
History	5	Mrs. Ballengee	Sewing (one semester)	6 (or 3 for year)	Miss Bell
Mathematics	5	Mrs. Ballengee	Study	1	
Oral English	1	Mrs. Ballengee			
Choral	2	Miss Brown	**Grade VIII**		
Physical Education	2	Miss Frederick	English	5	Miss Wallace
Hygiene	2	Miss Frederick	History	5	Miss Bolton

Subject	Periods per week	Instructor
Mathematics	5	Miss Judson
Oral English	1	Mrs. Ballengee
Choral	2	Miss Brown
Physical Education	2	Miss Frederick
Hygiene	2	Miss Frederick
Art	2	Miss Wing
Cooking (one semester) (or 3 for year)	6	Miss Auman
Sewing (one semester) (or 3 for year)	6	Miss Garrison
Study	1	

Grade IX

Subject	Periods per week	Instructor
English	5	Miss Wallace
Mathematics	5	Miss Judson
Typing (one semester)	6	Miss Catlin
Oral English	1	Mr. Ebey
Physical Education	2	Miss Frederick
Choral	2	Miss Brown
Art	2	Miss Wing
Cooking (one semester)	6 (or 3 for yr)	Miss Auman
Sewing (one semester)	6 (or 3 for yr)	Miss Garrison
General Science (one semester)	6	Mr. Ballengee
Study	2	

Grade X—General

Subject	Periods per week	Instructor
English	3	Miss Wallace
Journalism	2	Mr. Hudson
History	5	Miss Bolton
Mathematics	5	Miss Judson
Oral English	1	Mr. Ebey
Choral	2	Miss Brown
Physical Education	2	Miss Frederick
Art	4	Miss Wing
Home Hygiene	2	Miss Lill
Cooking (one sem. 4)	2 (1 year)	Miss Auman
Sewing (one sem. 4)	2 (1 year)	Miss Garrison
Study Period	1	

Grade X—Commercial

Subject	Periods per week	Instructor
English	3	Miss Wallace
Journalism	2	Mr. Hudson
History	5	Miss Bolton
Business Arithmetic	4	Miss Judson
Oral English	1	Mr. Ebey
Choral	2	Miss Brown
Physical Education	2	Miss Frederick
Typing	5	Miss Catlin
Home Hygiene	2	Miss Lill
Cooking (one sem. 4)	2 (1 year)	Miss Auman
Sewing (one sem. 4)	2 (1 year)	Miss Garrison
Study Period	1	

Grade XI—General

Subject	Periods per week	Instructor
English	5	Miss Wallace
Biology	5	Miss Judson

Subject	Periods per week	Instructor
History	5	Miss Bolton
Oral English	1	Mr. Shepardson
Choral	2	Miss Brown
Physical Education	2	Miss Frederick
Art	4	Miss Wing
Dietetics (one sem. 4)	2	Miss Hirleman
Sewing (one sem. 4)	2	Miss Garrison
Ethics	1	Mr. D. Bailey
Mothercraft	1	Miss Lill
Study	1	

Grade XI—Commercial

Subject	Periods per week	Instructor
English	5	Miss Wallace
Biology	5	Miss Judson
Oral English	1	Mr. Shepardson
Choral	2	Miss Brown
Physical Education	2	Miss Frederick
Dietetics (one sem. 4)	2	Miss Hirleman
Sewing (one sem. 4)	2	Miss Garrison
Ethics	1	Mr. D. Bailey
Mothercraft	1	Miss Lill
Study	1	Miss Catlin
Bookkeeping	4	Miss Catlin
Shorthand	5	

Grade XII—General

Subject	Periods per week	Instructor
English	5	Miss Wallace
History	5	Miss Bolton
Household Physics and Chemistry	4	Mr. Ballengee
Home Management (4-1 semester)	2	Miss Hirleman
Sewing (4-1 sem.)	2	Miss Garrison
Art	4	Miss Wing
Physical Education	2	Miss Frederick
Choral	2	Miss Brown
Oral English	1	Mr. Shepardson
Bible	1	Mr. D. Bailey
Study	3	Miss Judson

Grade XII—Commercial

Subject	Periods per week	Instructor
English	5	Miss Wallace
History	5	Miss Bolton
Household Physics and Chemistry	4	Mr. Ballengee
Home Management	2	(4 one sem) Miss Hirleman
Sewing (1 semester 4)	2	Miss Garrison
Physical Education	2	Miss Frederick
Choral	2	Miss Brown
Oral English	1	Mr. Shepardson
Bible	1	Mr. D. Bailey
Shorthand	4	Miss Catlin
Office Practice	3	Miss Moeller

SCHOOL FOR GIRLS STUDENT BODY OFFICERS
Left to right—Rebecca Macy, treasurer; Haunani Cooper, vice-president; Miss Marguerite Judson, adviser; Ellen Stewart, president; Dorothy Kahananui, secretary.

1934
BIG 6

Kamehameha School for Boys Student Leaders for 1934-35 (left to right) George West, who has counted among his school activities junior track, Quill and Scroll Honor Society, National Honor Society, Hi-Y, Christian Endeavor, band, Glee club, Rifle club, Ka Moi, Printing club; Hartwell Blake (the only high-

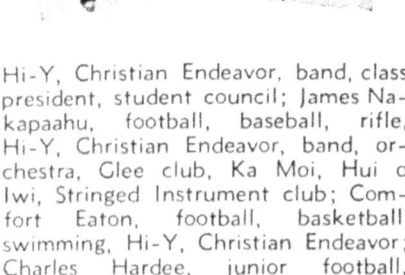

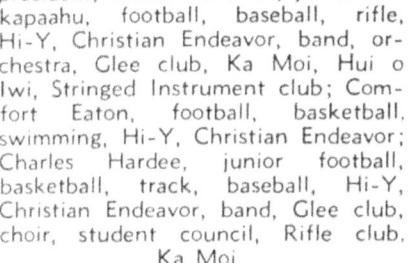

eleventh boy on the committee), football, track, baseball, swimming, rifle, Hi-Y, Christian Endeavor, band, Glee club, choir, student council, Hawaiian club, Quill and Scroll; Herbert Dunn, football, basketball, track,

Hi-Y, Christian Endeavor, band, class president, student council; James Nakapaahu, football, baseball, rifle, Hi-Y, Christian Endeavor, band, orchestra, Glee club, Ka Moi, Hui o Iwi, Stringed Instrument club; Comfort Eaton, football, basketball, swimming, Hi-Y, Christian Endeavor; Charles Hardee, junior football, basketball, track, baseball, Hi-Y, Christian Endeavor, band, Glee club, choir, student council, Rifle club, Ka Moi.

SCHOOL FOR GIRLS CLASS HEADS
Left to right—Mary Kunane, seniors; Dorothy Kahananui, juniors; Eleanor Horswill, sophomores; Margaret Clarke, freshmen; Winifred Cheong, eighth grade; Frances Nohoikaiu, seventh grade.

MANY STUDENT ACTIVITIES ARRANGED

Although they are on different campuses, there are many activities in which the boys and girls join together. Frequently Saturday nights are set aside for "calling." On those evenings the boys of the Senior High School Division may call on the girls. On the Kapalama campus the girls as hostesses always make this a pleasant evening with games and other social diversions for the boys.

Girls at the Senior Cottage from time to time invite students from the School for Boys for dinner, and Senior boys invite students from the School for Girls for dinner at K. S. B. During holiday seasons—Thanksgiving and Easter—when some of the students remain in school, boys and girls get together for dinner parties and games or dancing.

SCHOOL PAPER PUBLISHED BY STUDENTS

The school paper—Ka Moi—gives many of the boys and girls a pleasant outside activity. More than 80 students are members of the staff, while about 60 more take part as reporting classes. Special evening meetings are held to arrange the paper, which is a weekly, for publication. The big moment for these staff workers is the annual staff dance held each October. Members of honor societies and honor

---

Activities Occupy Pupils Outside Regular Classes

Program Includes Sports for Students, Clubs of Varied Interests, Music, and Several High Honor Organizations

---

students also attend this annual affair.

HONOR SOCIETIES REWARD ACHIEVEMENT

The Quill and Scroll Society is organized on the Kamehameha campus for those boys and girls who have done particularly good work in newswriting. This is an international honor society for high school journalists. The members arrange such things as special issues of Ka Moi, a special literary contest, and initiations for new members and occasional off-campus dinners.

Another honor society on the campus is the National Honor Society, which selects for membership those students who have been outstanding in their studies and in leadership. There is a chapter at K. S. G. and one at K. S. B.

DRAMATICS PART OF PROGRAM

It is lots of fun to take part in a play, and many boys and girls enjoy playing parts in the different plays presented at Kamehameha each year. In addition to the play usually put on in the spring by the Seniors there are a number of others given by various students during the year.

Sometimes very short skits are given for student programs. Occasionally the students wish to write their own short plays and do so. Sometimes these are

Publications activities. Left—Initiation of Quill and Scroll Honor Society members in Bishop Memorial Chapel; Right—Ka Moi, the student weekly newspaper, staff at one of its meetings.

given at assemblies. Students in the sewing classes are encouraged to help by making costumes; art students assist by planning scenery; special music numbers are given by music students; dancing classes contribute solo group numbers; the electric shop boys look after the lights; and so each boy and girl takes part according to his or her wishes and ability.

SPECIAL SCHOLARSHIP AWARDS

Special honor awards are made each term for the boys and girls standing high in their classes in scholarship and conduct. These awards are called Silver Pin Awards and are much prized. Sometimes it happens that a student makes an excellent record in all studies and in conduct, in which case that student receives a Gold Pin Award. For special improvement and ability in written and spoken English there are the Clarke English prizes of $10 each, awarded five times a year at the School for Boys and the School for Girls.

The School for Girls Stamp Club at an informal meeting.

Makua Albert F. Judd conducting the seniors on a tour of inspection through the Kamehameha Schools Hawaiian Forest.

1934 Kamehameha Football Squad

Junior and Inter-Scholastic Varsity

The Hi-Y clubs at the School for Boys include as part of their program the entering of teams in the city Hi-Y basketball leagues. Kamehameha boys have generally rated high in the all Hi-Y activities, frequently being elected to city-wide positions. The Christian Endeavor groups from the two schools get together occasionally for joint meetings in Bishop Memorial Chapel. The school has its own church organization, Bishop Memorial Church, which students may join if they wish or with which they may merely affiliate as associate members while retaining membership in their home churches. The Kamehameha church is non-sectarian.

TRADITIONS OF OLD HAWAII KEPT ALIVE

The traditions of old Hawaii are naturally of interest to Kamehameha Schools and a group of boys have organized a club for the definite purpose of keeping these traditions alive. This group—Hui Oiwi—has as one of its activities a special luau in the spring.

At the School for Girls those students interested in gardening have organized a Vegetable Garden Club which has raised and sold to the school many of the vegetables used in the K. S. G. dining hall.

STUDENT PARTIES PLANNED

Social activities in the spring include the military ball, the junior prom, and the senior class function. Movies are often shown the students, as the school has its own machines. In the fall before the football games the students get together in the K. S. B. gymnasium for rallies and make the rafters ring as they give way to their enthusiasm in support of the team.

HOOLAULEA POPULAR

Hoolaulea has become a day familiar

Sport in Hawaii of today; Kam beat McKinley 24 to 6 to win the 1934 grid title.

The School for Boys discussion group, Hui Anaina, which is conducted by the boys who investigate local and national or international problems and discuss them.

School for Girls pupils taking Christmas gifts for the less fortunate boys and girls.

to all Kamehameha people. To the growing group of alumni and alumnae it is of especial interest. Parents also enjoy the opportunity to visit the school and see the work their children are doing.

On this day the school holds open house for visitors and follows this up with an outdoor supper and, generally, an evening program. Not the least of the enjoyment of this occasion is the opportunity for old school friends to meet each other again.

ALUMNAE AND ALUMNI HAVE ORGANIZATION

The alumnae and alumni of Kamehameha are a particularly strong group. They are well organized and they carry through later years the "imua spirit" they gained in Kamehameha. They have their own regular meetings and sponsor various activities that show their live interest in their alma mater. To mention just one

Sport in olden days in Hawaii, a boxing match at Kealakekua, Hawaii.

Campfire Girls Club at the School for Girls gives the younger girls outdoor experiences and companionship.

thing, the Alumnae Association has raised funds to endow a scholarship in memory of Ida M. Pope, first principal of the School for Girls. From the income of this fund it is possible to help Hawaiian and part-Hawaiian girls continue their education. The younger graduates who have gone on to the University of Hawaii and elsewhere to schools of higher training have maintained a fine reputation for Kamehameha grads in athletics, scholarship, and the many other activities of college life.

KAM SPORTS TEAMS STRONG

Throughout her history the athletic teams representing Kamehameha have been a source of pride and satisfaction. Not all the teams have been winners—although a gratifying number of victories have come to the Blue and White—but all the teams have given their best.

SPORTSMANSHIP IMPORTANT

Sportsmanship means much to Kamehameha athletes and all their games are played with this ever in mind.

Kamehameha entered track and baseball competition back in the 1890's, one of her baseball teams defeat-

ing a visiting group of Big League baseball players from the mainland. In 1903 Kamehameha organized her first football team—and won the league championship. Since then Kamehameha has won seven more football titles, five of them in very recent years.

In the early 1900's the School for Girls engaged in basketball competition with other schools and was always known as a worthy opponent.

Basketball, soccer and other sports have been entered by the Kamehameha boys.

SPORTS FOR BOTH BOYS AND GIRLS

Today the School for Boys enters interscholastic and junior football, junior basketball, interscholastic track, and interscholastic baseball. Other occasional games besides regular league contests are played with various school teams.

The girls of today meet with girls of other schools sometimes for get-together play days.

CHRONOLOGICAL HISTORY OF KAMEHAMEHA

December 19, 1831 — Princess Bernice Pauahi born.

October 16, 1884—Mrs. Bishop died. Bulk of property willed to found Kamehameha Schools.

Junior division prize winners at the 1934 Halloween party.

October 20, 1887—Kamehameha School for Boys opened.

October, 1888—K. S. B. preparatory school was opened.

December 19, 1888—First Founder's Day celebrated.

June, 1891—First class graduated from Kamehameha Schools.

December 19, 1891—Dedication of Bishop Hall at School for Boys.

December, 1892—Course of study increased to six years.

October, 1894—Normal training work organized at Kamehameha—forerunner of territorial normal training work.

December 19, 1894—Kamehameha School for Girls formally opened.

June, 1897—First class graduated from Kamehameha School for Girls.

Song leaders of winning classes in the 1934 song contest at the Kamehameha School for Girls. Sarah Henrickson, left, with the Richards cup won by the ninth grade in the junior division.

Maile Cockett, center, has the New England Mothers cup, won by the senior class as senior division winner. Eunice Cockett, right, has the Maude E. Post cup, a new award presented by the students of the

Song leaders of the winning classes at Kamehameha School for boys in the 1934 song contest. David Alama (left) is holding the Trent cup awarded to the ninth grade as junior division victor and Kenneth Bell has the Andrews cup which went to the senior class as senior division winner.

School for Boys in memory of the former principal of the Preparatory School. This award was for the best original song.

December 19, 1897 — Bishop Memorial Chapel formally dedicated.

June, 1898—Agricultural work instituted at Kamehameha.

June, 1900—School for Boys and School for Girls placed under single administrative head.

November, 1903—First Kamehameha football team wins city championship.

December 13, 1904 — E. Faxon Bishop, present president of board of trustees, appointed to the board of trustees.

December 19, 1907—New manual training building at K. S. B. dedicated.

1908—Bishop Memorial Church organized.

1908—Regular army officer assigned to Kamehameha to have charge of military training.

April, 1918—Summer school shop course

at K. S. B. announced. Continued until 1924.

1922—Commercial training instituted at K. S. G.

June, 1924—First high school class graduated from Kamehameha.

September, 1924—Senior Practice Cottage arranged for girls.

Spring, 1925—First Hoolaulea.

1925—Part-time vocational training plan adopted.

September, 1925—Sheet metal and casting courses offered at K. S. B.

September, 1927—Weaving course introduced at K. S. G.

September, 1929—Leathercraft and bookbinding courses introduced at K. S. G.

September, 1931—K. S. G. moves to new campus on Kapalama Heights.

KAMEHAMEHA
SCHOOLS

STUDENT EXPENSES AT KAMEHAMEHA ARE LOW

What will it cost me to go to Kamehameha?

That is a very important question to the boy or girl planning to attend Kamehameha. And here is the answer:

The yearly fixed charges at Kamehameha Schools are $63.50, made up and payable as follows:

An initial payment of $23.50 is required upon admission in September and $5.00 on the first of each month of the school year thereafter.

For additional amount payable at registration in September, see charges for military and athletic uniforms below.

No reduction in any charges as above can be made for delayed entrance, for absence, for withdrawal, or in case of dismissal. Should the student desire individual instruction upon the piano, other instrument, or in voice, an additional annual charge of $20.00 will be made, payable in two installments of $10.00 each, in September and January, at the same time as tuition.

SUPPLIES AND INCIDENTALS

In addition to the fixed charges as above, supplies and incidentals for the school year are additional expenses, and accounts for such purchases are to be paid within the month in which they are due. Included in the amount estimated there is the cost of a uniform (for new students in the Boys' School) from, say, $15 for a good "secondhand" uniform if available, to $25 for a new uniform; an athletic uniform, required for all boys and girls, at $6; and books and school incidentals, averaging $20 for the first month and $5 to $10 each month thereafter. (Note: This does not include the student's spending money.) The payment for military and athletic uniforms is due with the registration fee in September.

The following are listed as approximate expenses for a year at the Kamehameha Schools:

BOYS' SCHOOL

Tuition	$ 50.00
Medical fee	5.00
Dental fee	5.00
School newspaper	2.50
Athletic fee	1.00
Dress uniform (secondhand)	15.00
Service uniform	10.00
Athletic uniform and shop trousers	6.00
Books	12.00
TOTAL	**$106.50**

GIRLS' SCHOOL

Tuition	$50.00
Medical fee	5.00
Dental fee	5.00
School newspaper	2.50
Athletic fee	1.00
Athletic uniform	6.00
Books	12.00
TOTAL	**$81.50**

This total includes food and lodging, but does not include laundry, toilet articles, and spending money. These items can be kept down if the student will use care; many boys have their laundry done at home and most of the girls do all their own laundry at the schools. Expenses for uniforms apply during the first year only; the school cannot guarantee to supply secondhand uniforms to all. New dress uniforms cost $25.00.

Day student charges are $15.00 less than charges for boarders; the tuition, including lunches, is $35.00 per year, instead of $50.00, and is payable $11.00 upon admission and $3.00 on the first of each month of the school year thereafter.

En. Fee 5.00
Lem. " — 5.00
Paper — 2.50
athletic " — 1.00
_____
13.50
tuition 50.00
$63.50 per year

$ 50.00 tuition per whole year
− 25.00 ½ tuition worked off per whole yr.
_____
$ 25.00 amt to be paid
+ 13.50 total amt of Fees
_____
38.50 amt. payable per whole school year
− 18.50 amt. paid
_____
20.00 amt. left to be paid monthly at 5.00 a month
or four payments to wipe off $20.00